What a Modern Catholic Believes About SEX

by

Eugene Kennedy

The Thomas More Press
Chicago, Illinois

Contents

WHAT A MODERN CATHOLIC
BELIEVES ABOUT SEX

F. S.

Introduction

WHAT THE CHURCH MEANT
TO TELL YOU ABOUT SEX
BUT NEVER GOT AROUND TO

SEX AND RELIGION, durable as death and taxes, have
traded places as conversational subjects in polite
society during the past century. Sex used to be taboo
but a certain form of pietistic religion was always acceptable. The situation really was not good for either
dimension of personality; now, however, the roles are
reversed. Sex is discussable everywhere while pietistic religion is in danger of being hooted out of any hall
except in the most fundamental evangelistic sections
of the country. A certain undeveloped form of religion
was described by Freud as the opiate of the people –
tranquilizing rituals that helped them to accept every-
day misery because of the good times that were coming.
Now sex, a new flowering of tyrannies based on half-
grasped theories rather than superstition, has become
the opiate of the masses, the great preoccupying,
uneasiness-generating, curiosity-whetting, and day-
dream-filling phenomenon of the moment.

Actually, real religion and real sex are closely related to one another. They are both sunk deep in man
just as they are both profoundly expressive of his true
strange Roman arena-like combat, although they have
been billed this way for a long time: a reliable main
attraction pitting the two battered gladiators of sex and
religion against one another in front of Shea Stadium-
like crowds. Men have felt the same kind of struggle
within themselves: sex and religion circling each other
like opponents who know nothing of each other but battle.

But religion and sex have a far more profound relationship than that of conflict. As vital aspects of growing persons they are meant to interrelate rather than clash with each other. Man's worst enemies, fear and ignorance, set them against each other because fear and ignorance are the perennial enemies of any kind of growth. They are the enemies of true religion and of genuine sexuality. Religion and sex are linked in the creative, sharing, and soul-revealing dynamics by which they make common cause for growth. They are not old enemies but ancient friends who, because of man's timidity and lack of knowledge, have become estranged from each other. In this same way both sex and religion have become outcasts from human personality and human relationships – Saturday's children disinherited by man who has felt empty and incomplete without them ever since.

Dr. David Reuben's recent book *Everything You Always Wanted to Know About Sex (But Were Afraid to Ask)* has at least the virtues of solid information and straightforwardness. It has been like a cool breeze for thousands of people tortured by misinformation and spurious legends about sexuality. Many of the same people have been driven by the spectres of guilt generated by a religion that has blurred its vision of man and the human condition. It is the aim of this book to put religion and sex back into relationship with one another by giving better information about both and by killing off the rumors and legends which, fed by ignorance and fear, have so estranged man from these profound aspects of his personality.

It is important, however, not to spend too much time lamenting the unfortunate sexual morality generated by certain religious and moral leaders in the past. These distortions have been well enough advertised and hardly need much repetition. I think, however, that it is important to supply what is notably lacking in many contemporary observations about sex: a moral reference point that uses something more than the pragmatic experience of pleasure as the yardstick for man's sexual activity. Sex is integral to man and must be seen in the light of his relationship to himself and his own potential as well as his relationship to other persons. Catholic moral theologians, I have come to be convinced, do not ply an enviable trade. It is difficult for them, in the present developing awarenesses of Christian theology, to treat concrete questions with as much certitude as their antecedent practitioners enjoyed. Any moral theologian is, after all, a guardian of our laws and ideals. Law is meant to refine the human experience of good people who earnestly try to live by the Gospel. A theologian tries patiently to keep up with the Christian community and the moral insights that arise in the course of the community's life experience. He must also test these against traditional formulations and descriptions of acceptable Christian behavior. The moral theologian, no matter what his own feelings, must deal gently with traditions no matter how out of date they are, for moral theology, among other things, is a gentleman's occupation. The moral theologian needs great patience as he tries to understand new human experience and man's more profound and subtle reflections on himself, especially when these seem to clash with what some teachers in the Church said in previous eras. But the theologian cannot write like a crusading newspaper editor nor shout like a fiery preacher. He attracts thunderbolts enough when he proposes even a tentative new formulation of some traditional Christian moral principle. He must try to support the integrity of the institutional aspects of the Church while he works the new experience into the mainstream of its life, knowing that what he understands in his own generation may not be wholeheartedly accepted until many years later. The present generation of moral theologians in the United States, men like

Charles E. Curran and Richard McCormick, are enormously skilled and deeply responsive to the needs of man and to the demands of the Church for a constantly developing understanding of moral principles. We can only be grateful to these men but we cannot expect them to put aside their scholarly discipline and ride point on the pilgrimage of the Christian community into the future.

One gets the impression that the moralists have moved as far as they can, for example, in discussing the question of birth regulation. Their struggle to place the question in the perspective of the experience of the Christian community leads them to speculate with great respect about the seeming lacunae in *Humanae Vitae,* to urge a very liberal and understanding mode of pastoral practice, and then to shift the argument to a different field of operation altogether. The theologians, in the name of liberating man, move away from him and his personal problems to a discussion that is of a more intramural flavor. The question has become one that is basically ecclesiastical: how do you fit *Humanae Vitae* into the life of the Christian community? So the debate rages, not about the original human issue but about what kind of document the encyclical is, fallible or infallible, and what kind of assent is proper to such a document, and, furthermore, can a Christian who is not an expert withhold consent to something the Pope says when he is explicitly taking on the role of teacher of faith and morals. Indeed, these theoretical questions arise because there appears to be a sharp conflict between this document and the convictions of many sincere Catholics. And the theologians have to try to live with both realities, giving support to the teaching authority of the Church even when they cannot quite believe it themselves.

One gets the impression that the big problem that now clouds the horizons of the Church centers on whether it is possible that the Church has made or is now making some kind of mistake that would be ruinous to its role as moral guide to mankind. Fathers Ford and Kelly put the problem well some years ago:

> . . . if the teaching of the Catholic Church on a point so profoundly and intimately connected with the salvation of millions of souls has been the same over such a long period of time, the inevitable conclusion must be that the teaching is true and unchangeable. Otherwise the Church which God established to interpret the moral law and to guide souls on the way of salvation would be failing substantially in its divine mission *(Contemporary Moral Theology,* Westminster, Maryland: The New Press, 1963, Vol. II, p. 258).

This kind of reasoning, of course, does not allow for new understandings of either man or theology; it is precisely this restricted viewpoint that has gotten the Church in a difficult position today. If we were to depart from the scholarly gentlemanliness of the current discussions, we might suspect that the problem comes down to this: how do we admit, at least in practice, that the Church may have made a mistake while maintaining at the same time that the Church cannot make this kind of mistake? So the search proceeds, reclassifying the status of papal documents, and reshuffling past ones in attempt to see if one or the other of these offers a basis in some tradition for a broader statement on birth regulation by the Church at this time. In other words, if somehow or other, it could be demonstrated that Pope Pius XI in *Casti Connubii* actually left room for a change in Church outlook while he was severely condemning birth control, then the theologians would have a way out of the present impasse. To the average man this is the kind of doubletalk that still leaves him to deal with his sexuality and all his life struggles as best

he can. While the discussion goes on many members of
the Christian community move forward, breaking
through the impasse on their own with a developing conviction that not all individual acts of birth regulation
can possibly be mortal sins *all* the time. These are
not impulsive or self-gratifying individuals, but sincere and open persons who care about right and wrong
in their relationships and who cannot afford to wait until
the theologians have sailed around the cape in pursuit
of a new passage to the truth.

In this book we will try, then, to listen to the Spirit
as it speaks in the experience of good people who constitute the Christian community and who want to do the
right thing in their personal lives. We must try to sense
in their experience now what will, in fact, inevitably be
expressed in law. The moral sense of good people is
positive, integrating, and ultimately humanizing of
themselves.

This is not, of course, to argue for a vote on Christian moral positions, nor for determining by poll-
results the morality of Christian sexual behavior. We
are not dealing with opinions or attitudes which may
shift like political inclinations from day to day; we are
concerned with convictions that have been burned free
of dross in the crucible of human experience. This is
not some shifting situational ethic in which the walls
contract or expand according to the strength of the
heartbeat of some vaguely defined love. A reliable
moral principle comes out of the interaction of people
who are mature in the judgment of most men and who
earnestly try, within the admittedly limited human condition, to make moral decisions which enlarge them as
persons. It is no easy wisdom, this sense of right and
wrong that governs sincere people who inform themselves as well as they can and reflect adequately on
their life situation. The Spirit is available to these
people and the Spirit speaks in the validation which

these good people give certain moral stands by their common judgment on them. There is never anything to fear in committing difficult moral questions to the judgment of well instructed and conscientious Christians. They always deal with situations according to the realism of their own lives and their answers are neither theoretical nor inapplicable. Good Christians can find a way that is within the reach of those motivated and strengthened by the Spirit.

Nothing is better entrusted to the judgment of the Christian community than the moral questions which affect their intimate lives with each other. Indeed, recent history tells us that when, on principle, these questions are kept from the judgment of the faithful and reserved to the theologians, enormous difficulties ensue. The clearest examples are cross-hatched with the values of religion and sexuality: celibacy and the question of birth regulation. There is a telling misplay and failure of confidence in the action of the Spirit in the Roman efforts to close off discussion on these sensitive and profoundly human subjects. But this kind of embargo on discussion fails in the modern world; the Christian community absorbs and reflects upon these questions even when the official spokesman of the Church would wish it otherwise. What has the Christian community already told us about these questions? We will try to share some of the answers that have already taken shape in the conscience of the contemporary Christian community.

You cannot talk about sexuality, or religion for that matter, unless you are sure of the image of man which is at the heart of your reflections. The Church is slowly recovering its understanding of man as an integral unit rather than as an awkward coupling of flesh and spirit held in relationship by the tension of some elemental conflict with each other. Divided man has been, however, the model for many of the moral decisions made about man and his sexuality over the past several centuries. You cannot really do right by man if you judge him as a fragmented creature rather than as a person striving for an ever finer integration of his own basic psychosomatic unity. The contemporary Church is in a good position to give back to the world an understanding of the person that is in accord with the Judeo-Christian tradition as precisely this unified being. The world is searching for a model on which it can rely for its understanding of man and for its ethical judgments about his present activity and his future goals.

The world is caught at the present moment between two inadequate models of man, each of which dominates a large trend in current counseling and psychotherapy. The first presents us with a superficial image of the human person. This is the notion of man who is a unity but who has little depth in either his understanding or in his emotional life. Concepts like love, trust, and truthfulness are bandied about with no sure sense of their profound connotations or the deep significance they have in the lives of persons who have achieved true psychological maturity. The superficial model of man uses the right vocabulary but cheapens it by selling man and his deepest values quite short. It is this model that inspires people to think that deep love can be generated in a marathon weekend, or that genuine trust will spring out of a few hours of sharing hidden truths with each other. This model has the right instincts but it does not have the full dimensions needed for a real understanding of man and his behavior.

Another view of man is emphasized by the psychotherapists who describe their task now as "behavior modification." Adopting the principles of conditioning, they claim to relieve man of his hangups, sexual and otherwise, with a minimum of difficulty and with no recourse to any kind of deep self-search or insight. They modify man's behavior by staying on the surface of his behavior, by blocking out any notions about man which come from anything other than looking at him from the outside. This stance does little justice to man because it leaves out so much of what gives lasting significance to his behavior. There is no moral referent when the treatment merely manipulates a person's emotional reactions without helping him to understand what lies beneath them. Behavioral modification becomes more popular every day because it cuts down on the length of treatment and claims a high record of success.

An odd thing about all scientists, physical and social, no matter where they are found: they frequently go ahead and do things to man without weighing the consequences. The greatest burdens and problems of the modern world arise precisely because of our failure to anticipate and deal with the long-term effects of certain things we have done, with unquestioned and impulsive certainty, to man and his environment. We set off atom bombs, pollute rivers, crowd the skies and suddenly realize that man suffers from all this. We do the same thing psychologically when we offer models of man to the world that simply do not measure up to the grandeur of the human person. Morality that does not sense man's profound meaning is no morality at all and, if it seems liberating in one generation, it may be enslaving in the next.

The Christian vision of man does not see sexuality as an easy response that enables him to transfer trust at an afternoon workshop. Neither is this sexuality merely one aspect of his behavior, which can be changed or modified to remove anxiety. The Christian model of man sees human sexuality, with all that it reflects and expresses, as integral to his full human presence in the world. Sexuality is not perceived as something adjunctive, nor as some kind of erotic seasoning which encourages man to keep the race alive.

In the long run, the Christian view of man sees sexuality as rooted in his experience of relationship to himself, his neighbor, and to God. It is linked, in other words, with the religious dimension of personality which, when it is fully developed, gives man a viewpoint from which he can see himself and judge his behavior in terms of whether it contributes to his own growth and to that of his neighbor. Christian moral judgment leads men to life; the journey to new life is the journey to resurrection and there is no way to get there without facing the thousand deaths of love and life.

In the behavior that surrounds man's sexuality we find all the elements of his struggle to find his own identity and to reach out in sharing it with others. In this book we will try to deal with the pertinent questions connected with man's sexuality as he passes through all the stages of his life. We will try to understand the kind of judgment that is being made now through the experience of the growing Christian community on the questions that have troubled men and moralists endlessly. We will try to put to flight the fear and ignorance which have kept the Church, in some ways at least, from teaching mankind everything it really doesn't know about sex.

Chapter One

THERE WERE NO GOOD OLD DAYS

I N NO AREA of human life is it less appropriate to look back at a supposedly more innocent and virtuous past than in the area of man's sexual behavior. Concerned observers, noting the pervasive sexuality of our times, say that things have changed, that things have gotten worse, especially in our sexual morality. Hard as it may be for those who enjoy moral indignation to accept, it is difficult to defend this thesis. Things may be bad now but they are the same things that were bad in the last century and in the centuries before that. As a matter of fact, many values connected with sexuality have improved considerably. There is no splendid untrammelled sexual past in the memory of any man or in the records of any culture. Contemporary man has, if anything, been making a little progress in understanding himself and the meaning of his sexuality. There is nothing, literally nothing new under the sun as far as sexual behavior goes. The big difference is that now it is in fact under the sun. All the behavior connected with and expressed through man's sexuality has a long, diverse, and extremely complicated history.

Nothing fascinates man more than his sexuality and, whether he chooses to talk about it or maintain a repressed silence, he has indulged in an incredibly wide range of sexual behavior with a spirit of persistence and invention throughout history. The so-called new permissiveness has not given rise to any really new forms of sexual behavior. Nor is there evidence that it has made man less moral. It has, if anything, made man more aware of himself and the sexual components of his human nature; it has confronted him with the problem of understanding what the many forms of his sexual behavior are all about.

Some aspects of what is occurring now are clearly healthy. Man has moved over the centuries toward a more profound understanding and appreciation of marriage as centered on the personal relationship between man and woman. Man has also become far more attuned to his own sexuality and has become, with the mixture of energy, sincerity, and curiosity that moves him in all his most important projects, to understand his own sexuality. And man has come to a deeper appreciation of woman even though Woman's Lib would say that this has been too little, too late, and, as yet, not enough. The arc of this swing, which represents a movement away from sexuality as an animal activity confined to certain aspects of the body toward an understanding of sexuality as a human activity symbolizing and expressing the union of persons, has been sweeping indeed. A heavy price has been paid for a more refined understanding of man and the significance of his sexuality. The toll is heaviest on the institutions which carved out their main features in years which had less appreciation of the overall personal values which undergird a Christian understanding of sex. These institutions, including marriage itself, are challenged, not because of rampant immorality but because of a heightened evaluation of the essential marriage relationship. This has put a strain on the structures around marriage; these are groaning and cracking because far more weight is put on them by the high demands man and woman make on each other for emotional fulfillment in marriage. This stress, documented by divorce statistics, arises because marriage is no longer emphasized solely as an institution necessary for the continuation of the human race. When marriage was understood as an institution rather than as a personal relationship, the couple expected less from each other and consequently were not nearly so disappointed.

It is difficult to find any period in the history of civilization to which we could confidently point as the location of the practice of an advanced morality from which we have now scandalously fallen. Surely it cannot be found in the eras during which women were considered property and where a man's morality was frequently determined more by his socio-economic class than by anything else. Tremendous variations in sexual morality have always been witnessed across various levels of education and socio-economic status. It is, as a matter of fact, true to this very day. You cannot find heightened morality even in puritan New England. Behind the tightlipped expressions of the Pilgrims who seemed to celebrate the first Thanksgiving so nobly and chastely danced the same kind of fantasies and thoughts that you find in men's minds today. The stern sexual code of the Puritans, for all its floggings and brandings, did not seem to make for a well-ordered morality in the early colonies. The Church records in Groton, Connecticut, for example, tell us that between the years 1761 and 1775 the parents of one third of the baptized children made public confession (to save the child from perdition) of having had premarital intercourse. That is not a bad statistic to remember for anyone who bewails excessively the present-day trend in the same direction. The golden age of sexual morality is not to be found in the English-speaking world, not even in the South in the days of supposed chivalry, where the double standard allowed unparalled freedom to white men in their exploitation of Negro women. In fact, as Robert M. Frumkin has noted in "Early English and American Sex Customs" (*The Encyclopedia of Sexual Behavior*, Hawthorn Books, 1961, p. 363), that for the 1350 years surveyed in his article the following conclusions are appropriate:

1. Sex was regarded as a necessary evil, its only

        justification being procreation and the mainte-
nance of male immortality.

2. Woman was the incarnation of evil because she
was "sex." She was necessary as the "soil" in
which the male "seeds" grew, and her main func-
tion was essentially that of a breeding animal.

3. Marriage was a civil contract, a business whose
purpose, as perpetuated by the Calvinistic Puritans, was to acquire wealth and property, in order
to determine whether one was among the saved or
the damned.

4. Sexual repression was the everlasting order of
the era . . . women were always more repressed
than men, for a double standard in favor of men
generally prevailed. Arrests, punishments for
female sexual offenders were consistently more
severe than for male offenders.

There is not an even road on the whole horizon. What
we can say is that at the present time, because of increased knowledge and sensitivity to man and his nature, there is at least a struggle toward a more informed Christian sexual ethic. Man, under tremendous
pressures, is trying to get himself together as *the*
human person in whom sexuality is better understood
and valued than ever before in history. The point of
these observations is that we must see man's struggle
for sexual integrity in the context of his overall personal growth. The mistake has always been to put too
much emphasis on sex as separated from the other
aspects of man's yearnings and his potential. It is
immoral to misunderstand and distort his sexuality by
severing it from the conditions of growth which man
needs to develop fully. It is hypocritical to silence
those who ask questions that must be answered, even
when the questions give rise to anxiety in ourselves
because they touch on sexual matters. It is immoral
to move backward, speaking with longing about a past

that never existed, when the Christian community is attempting to move forward, to secure new understandings of man and to open itself for even more sensitive understandings in the future. It is immoral to settle for a veneer of behavior which merely covers up a wide range of deviant sexual activity. This latter charge is precisely the one that has been hurled at older generations by youth. They realize that there were no good old days and they cannot abide the seeming hypocrisy which tries to control their behavior while it maintains a double standard for the older generation. There is a lot that is wrong with youth but in no place are they more accurate in their indictment of the older generation than in their clear view of our own failure to deal more maturely with our sexuality and the moral questions connected with it. It is no wonder that people are shouting, clamoring at the barricades, raising a howl in an undignified way. We wish they would be more polite and that they would state their questions with dignity. But better they shout than that they accept the kind of silence that has prevented man from facing the truth about the centuries of difficulty he has had with sexuality. Their cry is, "I am human and I want to understand myself." And it is in understanding this demand that we can formulate some sensible Christian morality about sex in our own day.

It is clear that the new expressions of Christian morality have moved away from the application of a grid of categorized decisions based on purely theoretical considerations of man's behavior. The Christian community now carefully examines human experience with an effort to be sensitive to the individual's concrete moral problems. This is part of the transformation of the methodology of Catholic moral theologians described by the late John Courtney Murray as a shift from a classicist to a more historically conscious methodology. This is not a shift to totally subjective morality but it does indicate the contemporary effort to appreciate man's individual struggle rooted in a certain time and place. It means that the morally concerned must work to understand his obligations in the ever-shifting real situations of his life. This is far different from thinking about what man ought to be like and applying pre-conceived judgments without qualifications to every moral question that arises.

Christian morality is nowhere better applied than to man's sexual behavior. There is nothing that will clear the head of an intellectualizing theologian more than some face-to-face contact with the way men and women tend to behave precisely because they are sexual beings. Theology is moving swiftly away from neat boxes derived from some ideal notions about man toward a confrontation with man as he is and, as far as historical records seem to indicate, always has been in his sexual behavior.

It is quite clear, for example, that many of the sexual activities of the human race could better be understood as immature rather than as immoral. It is much more helpful to weigh man's sexual activity on the scales of growth rather than on the scales of right and wrong. This is a very difficult business to achieve, filled as it is with temptations to rationalize away practically everything on psychological grounds. This danger is no doubt present, but it is not nearly so serious a problem as the danger of misjudging man because we do not understand the way human beings grow and develop. In many situations the focus has been exclusively on sexual behavior rather than on the antecedent cultural conditions which give rise to certain forms of sexual behavior in the first place. For example, it is rather a simple thing to categorize the sexual behavior of soldiers into what is right and what is wrong. They are famous, as are most men forced for whatever reason to live and survive without women for long periods of

time, for their freebooting sexual morality. While it is
easy to say that this, measured against an ideal standard, is wrong, it looks quite different when we put it
back into the context of war itself, with its extreme
pressure on each individual to cope with a world filled
with unreason, blood, and sudden death. What do men
do to keep from going mad in circumstances that are
quite mad themselves? They do extraordinary things,
many of them cruel and disordered, some of them ap-
palling as far as the normal standards of sexual behavior go. The point is, however, that these behaviors
are, in a very real sense, the average person's efforts
to solve the problems that come from being caught up
in a terrifying and disfigured world in which whatever
human pleasure and comfort he can find, no matter how
short-termed, may be urgently necessary to hold his
humanity together. The gross immorality lies in war
and the desperate things it does to men who try to survive in its landscape of flame and smoke. The moral-
ist's interest cannot be just to prevent or describe the
immorality of soldiers; it must obviously be directed
toward the dehumanizing conditions which push men
into situations in which ordinary moral laws are difficult to apply. What is needed for an authentic moral
outlook in this and other similar situations is something different from a readiness to judge the rightness
or wrongness of an individual's sexual behavior. A
compassionate understanding of the ways that men adjust and try to make sense out of life when their days
are full of death is far more important than applying a
moral textbook's categories to men at war.

The same should be applied to other groupings;
over-mortgaged suburbanites, for example, or men
caught in the widely described pressures of techno-
logical society. What man does in these circumstances
turns out to be what he has always done in the course
of history when he has had to search out and hold on to

something as a sign of his humanity. This may come out in very distorted forms but the sexual nature of much of man's adjustive behavior is at least a sign of man's groping, in an understandable human way, for something to keep him in touch with himself and with other persons. To put man into finer focus, as we might in the terrible circumstances of war, is not merely to loosen the bonds of sexual morality so that, if we can make a good enough case for it, anything goes. When we get a clearer picture of man and the major role sexual symbolism has in telling us about him and his efforts to adjust to the world, we can see the importance of an informed Christian attitude toward the human person that is basic to any kind of effective sexual morality in our day. Indeed, it is only when we can make room in our perceptions of man's life-space for him to be truly human that we can help him to confront more truly the nature of the moral choices he must make in a wide variety of life circumstances. Unless, in other words, we have an appreciation for the full dimensions of man's freedom in his earthly condition, we cannot help man to exercise the kind of self-restraint and self-discipline that go along with a purposeful human and moral life. Unless we assist man to work through the immature stages of his growth, he can never really arrive at the fully developed moral choice that is possible only with psychological maturity. This attitude also enables us to help man see the depths of his own being and appreciate, with something more than theory, the richness and sacredness of human personality. Without a sense of this, morality is merely a shallow exercise that does not match the true nature of man.

This attitude of taking human beings seriously as individuals, with distinct genetic inheritance and very different life histories, is the key to speaking about sexual morality in a way in which man can understand. Two trends are clearly observable in the contemporary effort to understand man's sexuality in an historical and psychological context. These may be characterized as the person-centered and the self-centered approaches.

In the self-centered approach, pleasure becomes the yardstick by which sexual morality is judged as appropriate or inappropriate to man. If it gives pleasure, if it doesn't hurt anybody, and if nobody else knows about it, the proponents of this view seem to say: "Well, why not?" This self-centered attitude is based on a more compassionate view of man and a deeper understanding of the fact that certain sexual activities such as masturbation are not necessarily sinful. It does not, however, view man according to the dimensions of his growth potential; neither does it differentiate the various levels of immaturity that are associated with human sexual activity. There is no moral referent aside from the notion of pleasure. While this seems a highly liberated attitude, it ends up turning man in on himself because it fails to see him in adequate relationship either to himself or to other persons.

The person-centered view understands man and his potential for growth to the fullness of human individuality. This perception of man does not automatically disown pleasure but it places it in the perspective of man's other relationships and responsibilities. The person-centered view of man does not focus too much on any one aspect of behavior but rather tries to interpret all behavior in relationship to the ultimate meaning of the person. This view also understands human growth as being rooted in relationships with other persons. Relationships provide the setting for morality and for sexual morality in particular because this is where responsible behavior toward each other shows up in the human condition. Love becomes a real measure of morality, but not as some spongy romantic kind of phenomenon; the heightened sense of responsibility toward each other essential to real love enables us to see our moral decisions in sexual matters in a much clearer light.

The basic moral question thus boils down to what we think about man and what we hope for man. Man is growing and has reached a certain point where, with a new sensitivity to himself and a new freedom from a more repressive and ineffective moral code, he can decide whether he wants to become more or less human in the future. Never in history has it been possible for man to see and understand his sexual behavior as clearly as it is today. There is no past golden age to which he can return. His sexual behavior has always been expressive of his human nature. Now that he understands this better, he can face up to individual decisions about sexual morality with a keener sense of his own freedom and his own destiny.

True reverence for life emerges when we interpret man and the meaning of his sexuality with an understanding we have never before possessed. Man may not be better than he ever was but he is surely not worse. He now faces the moral decisions about his sexuality with a better appreciation of all that his own sexuality means and the way in which it is a sign of his profound moral behavior as a truly responsible human being. Twentieth century man can weigh his actions, their motivations and their consequences, in a way that his ancestors never could. The present deepest moral choice is whether man will choose fullness of life, with all the intricate moral problems associated with concrete reality, or whether he will choose something less than this and, therefore, something less than what is appropriate for him as a human person. The Church's task is to bring an essential understanding of the person and his destiny to man together with a determination to struggle compassionately with him as he makes these decisions about his future.

Chapter Two

SEX AND THE GROWING PERSON

SEX HAS suffered greatly from being cut off from the rest of life. There is nothing new about this problem except for the fact that we are becoming more aware of it and are presently trying to do something about it. The awareness of the tragedy of the separation of sex from the context of human growth and development is painful because it enables us to see how much damage and needless suffering it has brought to people. Until we can truly – and not just theoretically – understand sex as integral to man's personality and closely related to and expressive of his overall development, we will understand neither man nor his sexuality because our images of both will be fragmented and incomplete. So too our moral wisdom or sense of what is right or wrong for growing man will also be fragmented and incomplete.

There is no doubt that many contemporary cultural sources contribute to the isolation of sex from its proper context in human personality. The world is filled with examples of sex that has been cut off at its human roots: the innumerable liaisons that come under the rubric of "having sex;" the explosion of voyeuristic-lets-keep-real-people-at-a-distance-sex; the insatiable narcissism about one's technique or performance; the banners, billowing in the mind's eye like the great swastika streamers over the eager Teutonic crowds of the thirties, saying, "Take what you can get while you can." To these and other manifestations of cultural immaturity must, however, be added the tendency of theologians to treat sex in the same separatist way over the centuries. It has been particularly difficult for Catholics to get sexuality back into perspective because so much attention was paid to individual sex-related acts without much reference to the context of human growth and development. Indeed, the very notion that you can't make sense out of sex if you don't keep the right image of man in mind seemed not to be fully understood by moral theologians. In fact it is only during the last generation that they have begun to learn from the sciences that explain man.

We are, however, in a time of healing and insight, and this period, like all times of readjustment, is a very difficult one for everybody concerned. Moral theology, as mentioned before, is a gentleman's game and the rules must be observed with care by even the most enlightened scholars if their works are to have any positive influence. They must examine all former opinions, treating even the obviously horrendous with the deferential vocabulary of scholarship ("This opinion would seem inconclusive" . . . "It is difficult to sustain this position" . . . "it is perhaps no longer wise to assert") and God be good to them for their patience. The modern moral theologian also points toward the Christian experience, the moral wisdom that comes from the actual fact of the community's reflections on its own life, and looks to this for the actual process of re-integrating sex as a living aspect of man in healthy relationship to himself and to his neighbor. The theologian is able to open up the way be clearing the irrational debris that has fallen across man's path from various ivory towers, but man must move forward into the freer situation of adult living if the re-integration of his sexuality is to be complete. To do this he needs a fundamental sense of the Gospel values about man and an image of human personality that is sturdy and multi-dimensioned enough to reflect what he himself is truly like. The present generation of Catholics has not been liberated from ancient and inadequate codes of sexual behavior merely to enjoy some kind of stark raving erotic freedom. The sincere Catholic is joined with the theologian and every other serious person in the search to put himself and his sexuality back together again so that man can achieve his true growth as a human being.

The essential concept is growth, that mysterious and exhilarating characteristic, now shifting, now silent, now edged with excitement and now draining us like a summer sun, that hard-to-define condition of human life that constantly explodes the prisons of words and preconceptions that we build around man. Nothing is truer of man than that he is born to be on the move, to make his way through a series of increasingly demanding relationships to the fullness of his personality. Man is not, in other words, static; you can't see him with the eye of Matthew Brady and his Civil War photographic equipment that could only record a man who held himself awkwardly still; you see him better through the eye of a modern movie director with cameras and editing that capture the living qualities of man by not asking him to hold still at all. Any sexual morality based on a rigid and fixed notion of man is inadequate because it simply doesn't catch man the way he is; it offers a devitalized version of him at best. We need then to look more closely at growing man, sensing the stages of his passage through life, and seeing his sexuality veined into his personality at every moment. This will enable us to understand sexual difficulties in relationship to man's overall development and to relate our Gospel values to this process rather than to any isolated moment in it.

Many of the great figures who have looked deeply into man in order to understand rather than judge him have described the dynamic patterns of personal growth. Freud spoke of various levels of development related to certain parts of the body which seemed to be more significant as the individual progressed through life. Piaget has presented carefully described and progressive periods of intellectual development. Perhaps the schema that has received most attention recently is that offered by Erik Erikson of Harvard. He describes eight stages of psychosocial development, somewhat more literary than scientific in origin and language, but extremely helpful in understanding man and the process of his personal growth. Erikson presents man as capable of growth throughout the life cycle. This growth is related at each stage to the important persons in his life. Erikson also describes specific crises which the individual must meet and work through at each stage in order to achieve the human values and characteristics which he needs to proceed on to the next stage. We will review these briefly here, pointing to them as helpful descriptions of the developing human context in which man's sexuality is challenged, develops, and is expressed. Other people are important at each stage and so they are whenever we consider man's sexuality. Sexuality never exists just by itself and neither do sexual problems. Sexuality is not adjunctive but essential to man. Man moves through life, growing throughout its cycle, and he does this altogether, sexuality included, or we do not have man at all.

We will review Erikson's conceptions briefly, indicating some of the specific sexual problems and challenges that we will then consider in subsequent chapters.

Stage One: The First Year of Life

During this year the most significant other person in the child's life is the mother or, if she is absent, whoever takes her place. The way this person relates to the child will determine in many ways the child's whole attitude of trust or mistrust of the world around him. This is not to exclude the possibility of modifications of the child's attitude by later experiences but it highlights the very fundamental nature of the learning that takes place at this stage. A fundamental grasp of what it means both *to get* and *to give* takes place at this stage.

There are serious questions, often obscured by fear and ignorance, that are closely related to sexuality at this stage. These include the manifestations of infant sexuality and some of the basic attitudes and behaviors of the mother that may influence strongly the child's understanding of himself as male or female. Failure of trust and fear are infectious diseases at this stage and more than a little damage has been done to children by elders who have not dealt straightforwardly with their responsibilities at this level.

The infant's experience of the world and other persons as trustworthy or not strongly shapes, for good or for ill, enduring attitudes that he or she will bring into all other later life relationships. This first stance of trust or mistrust will profoundly affect the person's ability to express sexuality in a healthy and appropriate manner. Here is a clear example of a fundamental human milieu which, because of its impact on all behavior, must be appreciated sensitively by anyone trying to understand human sexuality.

Stage Two: Through the Second Year

The child has developed enough to control his own movements and with this mastery of self a whole new sense of individuality awakens. His sense of autonomy, of what we can call self-control and willpower, develops in the context of his relationship with both parents. If the child is mishandled (not allowed to do what he can do, or if he is overprotected) he may be dominated by a sense of shame and doubt instead of a healthy sense of autonomy.

Here again, issues connected with childhood sexuality, and the parents' own sexual feelings, some of which can be very complicated, are highly important.

Much that is essential for impulse control is learned at this level. That this is significant for a person's understanding and mature possession of his own sexuality is obvious. The *do's* and *don'ts* of later life may not mean much to an individual who has never taken charge of himself.

Stage Three, From Three to Six

The child, now related to the basic family, is in control of many of his actions at this stage. The outcome of his challenge here is the achievement of a sense of healthy initiative which will animate his attitude of direction and purpose in life. The child, probing his environment, must be taken seriously or he may find that a sense of guilt outweighs any initiative toward life. In other words, he will be freed in some way to move forward confidently, or he may be burdened by a confining sense of guilt.

The same questions of childhood sexuality exist at this stage and the sensitivity with which they are handled continues to be crucial. There is more concern here for masturbation and for the way in which response is made to the child's curiosity about sexual matters. Deeper than all this, of course, is the child's apprehension of what it means to set and achieve a goal, a kind of learning basis to later stability of his whole psychological life.

Fourth Stage: From Six to Puberty

The child moves into a wider arena of life at this period; the neighborhood and the school are new worlds for him. He achieves a level of intellectual development that allows him to see his environment, with its games and tasks, in a more comprehending way. Now he must develop a sense of industry, a feeling that he can make things, and that he can participate with others in a competitive and a cooperative manner. Failing in this, he will experience a pervasive sense of inferiority.

The awakening child will have, almost inevitably, experiences during this time which will have a clear sexual aspect to them. The manner with which these are treated by the parents will be continuingly important for his development, as will the relationship of the mother and father with each other. This latter relationship is extremely significant throughout the growing child's life and many questions about the sexual aspect of the parents' behavior should be clear to themselves at this time. The child's sense of confidence in himself will naturally affect his later attitudes toward his or her sexuality.

Fifth Stage: Adolescence

One hardly needs to describe the dynamic quality of the growing individual's life experience at this stage. During this time the person draws together the strands of his life experience to form his own identity. Either he develops a sense of unique self or he experiences confusion because of the diffuse quality of self-understanding at this time. The person's peer groups and leadership figures become important to him. He also begins to deal with profound human values, values that touch on the way he presents himself to the world and to other persons. For it is at this stage that he must develop a sense of fidelity and devotion to others.

Many experiences of a sexual nature will occur at this time. Not all of adolescence need be a terrible storm if parents have interacted successfully with the child at the levels below this. Certain questions, however, will have obvious importance. The answers to these are not just factual but also attitudinal; the authenticity or hypocrisy of the parents will be searched out and their true attitudes toward sexuality will be significant for many of the judgments of the young person makes both about them and the manner in which he will now possess his own personality, including his sexuality, in relationship to others. The problems of dating, pre-marital sex, and continuing questions of masturbation will come up at this time. The overall sense of personal identity and the appreciation and practice of fidelity are of paramount importance for the individual's sexual expression throughout all his life.

Sixth Stage: Early Adult

Here the young person takes his identity and tests it in relationship to others in a deeper way than he has done before. He must learn the meaning of intimacy as he moves either closer to others in friendship and love, or away from them in some kind of psychological isolation. At this stage the meaning of love as a lasting value and motivation come into his life as he faces the experience of losing and finding himself in relationship with another.

It is clear that the previous stages of life have brought the person to the point of mature development where his sexuality can have extraordinary significance if its growth is in harmony with the rest of his personality. All the questions about responsible sexual activity in mature loving relationships are relevant at this stage.

Seventh Stage: Young And Middle Adult

Here the individual has joined himself in love with

another for the mature tasks of building a family and passing life and growth on to others. The individual will become truly generative in the sense that he has an active and genuine concern for the generations that follow (for the consequences, in other words, of his work and love), or he turns away in self-absorption, letting the meaning of life slip by.

The continuing problems of personal growth at this stage have their counterpart in the sexual concerns of people who have responsibilities for the good of their own children and the good of the world around them. Serious questions about birth-control, abortion, and divorce arise at this stage. Other issues that reflect and express themselves in sexuality, e.g. the sudden awareness of getting older, are also present.

Eighth Stage: Later Adult

This is the level of putting one's life together in a reflective way. The major achievements of an individual are behind him; he must sum it all up, viewing it with a sense of integrity or, if there have been major flaws, with a possible sense of despair.

The whole question of the integrated personality cannot exclude the sexual dimension, which, for many is still quite active. Also present, of course, are problems connected with the aging process, changes that affect a person's whole outlook on the integrity of life. A person must ask whether he has spent his existence well now that he is coming closer to the outer border of life itself. The full realization that manhood or womanhood has been fruitfully lived out in all its dimensions enables a person to deal with this closing phase of life.

Nobody can tear sex out of this framework of human growth and think they are dealing with the subject as it comes up in human experience. Sex comes up at all these levels as does its true significance as an indication of a person's whole moral presence in life. The way a man identifies himself includes his sexuality or he has an unreliable sense of himself and, despite whatever defense he may use, a shaky way of relating himself with other people. Most of the problems of growth will reveal themselves in one way or another in the sexual dimension of a person's life. What becomes important is not just the sexual activity in itself, with all the oohing and ahhing we may do about it, but an understanding of the person who is the author of the activity. You name it, from adultery to zoophilia, and you cannot pronounce moral judgment on it unless you can see very deeply into the individual's life history. Take again the example of sexual identity, a not uncommon difficulty in contemporary America. When a man is unsure of himself as a person he may go about proving his masculinity over and over again. That means he has not worked through a crisis of growth that should have been handled at the adolescent level of his development. Now his solutions, through feigned aggressive sexuality, point beyond their immediate expression to the real source of the difficulty. It is wrong for a person to manipulate women and use them to reassure himself of his masculinity. There is no doubt about it. But there is a more fundamental wrong in the failure of those responsible for the growth and education of the individual to assist him in working through the parent problem at the right stage in life. His sexual morality expresses his immaturity, his continued struggle for some kind of solution to his diffused sense of self. There is no easy way to overlook this chain of events, no way to cut the individual out of time and space so that one does not have to take account of this.

Some complain that psychology tries to take away sin by involving us in complicated explorations for the sources of an individual's actions. In some ways this is true. Many of the things that have been called sins, especially in the realm of sexual behavior, are not sins at all. They are the signs of man's difficulties in growing, difficulties that are only made worse when he is not helped to see what his trouble is but is instead harassed by the spectre of multiplied guilt. Our fundamental moral concern must be with the setting of a person's life, with the circumstances in which he gets his first ideas about himself, life, and the whole set of moral values that will define his style of relating to other people. A Catholic's concern is with developing a world that lives by the Gospel values that, in the long run, alone can insure the human family of an environment in which it can achieve personal and moral maturity. And Christian sexual morality must be rooted in this human setting if it is to have any reliability and consistency. It is in this direction that the new generation of moral theologians are leading us, but they need the help and support of everyone who has a genuine feeling for the way man grows and develops into moral personhood.

In closing, it might be noted that any agency concerned with man's moral behavior should devote most of its energies not to tracking his sinful steps but to building a society in which the Christian values will enable men to achieve the fullness of personal growth that is necessary for healthy and mature morality. The Church should lead in this movement. Its business is not sin but virtue, not death but life, not what cripples a man but what helps him to be free. We are at last moving out of the era where any talk about sex was considered indecent and improper. We Catholics are discovering again our heritage that bids us to celebrate life and the conditions man needs to achieve it. (We are not the only ones. Many Protestants are climbing down from their Puritan towers to find that the earth is sweet and is strong enough to hold man. That they have really been estranged from man is evidenced in the recent behavior of Harvey Cox who, discovering that life is not all grey and grim, has been given to wearing vestments, celebrating in the streets, and saying embarrassingly immature things like, "Both blood and sperm are explosive, irregular, feeling-pitched, messy and inexplicably fascinating." It shows up in sex, like we said.)

It is with a sense of where our emphasis must go to build a sexual morality that matches man that the following dialogue chapters are presented. They will not settle every question, but they should make us look in the right direction.

Chapter Three

INFANCY

Q. *Can we really talk about sexuality being a factor in the life of a baby?*

A. There is plenty of evidence to support our understanding of sexuality in infants. It was once felt that it was immoral to suppose that this could be true and indecent even to speak about it. The presence of sexuality in the infant and the influence of sexual factors in his overall environment are, however, realities that can hardly be ignored. Our attitude toward this area of human sexuality is most important. In fact it is indecent and immoral not to speak of the influence of sexuality both for the sake of the child and also for the sake of the man and woman who are husband and wife as well as parents.

Q. *What do you mean about there being sexuality in the environment of the child?*

A. I refer to several factors that have to do with the way the parents express themselves as human beings in relationship to the child. There is a sexual component in most of our activities but it is surely present in an influential way in the relationship between a mother and a child. It is also significant in the continuing relationship of the husband and wife to each other. There are many subtleties to this and the birth of the child will have a profound effect, with sexual reverberations, on the parents.

Q. *What are some of the important things as far as the mother is concerned during this first year of the child's life?*

A. The *manner* of the mother's relationship is very important at this time. The way she looks at the child, that is, whether she perceives the child as a new person with rights and a budding individuality of its own, or whether she looks at the child as an extension of herself, or in some other non-personal way, will set the stage for the infant's psychosexual development. The studies of the development of gender identity indicate that the mother's attitude can be crucial even at this early time in the infant's life. In other words, the mother's whole stance will start the child moving toward a mature self-identification as a man or a woman or it can interfere notably with this, giving rise to serious psychological problems. That, of course, is not what happens in good, healthy households. But anybody who does not think that this early communication between mother and child is important has really not thought the question through very well.

Q. *You mention something about the relationship of the husband and the wife who are also the mother and father.*

A. Yes, there are very real demands on the parents to give during this first year of the infant's life. They really do not get much back at this stage. A young husband and wife, with no previous experience with children, have almost as much growing to do as the child himself. This affects their whole adjustment, including their sexual relationship. They must, after all, adjust to a new person with which each of them has a separate relationship. A husband and wife must help each other to become a father and mother during this significant period both in their lives and in the life of their child. Too little emphasis has been put on the significance of the husband-wife relationship, the health of which, however, has such a profound effect on the way the infant will develop.

Q. *You seem, however, to emphasize the woman's role during this first year of life?*

A. That's right, the world of the child is largely that which he inhabits with his mother, hence the great significance of the mother's role. It is a difficult and delicate role for her to carry on. She must feel free enough to give generously of her love to the child. She must, however, do this by extending her identity to be truly physically present to the child but in a way that does not exclude the father. A very serious problem often arises at this time when the mother, even without knowing it, can shift with the center of gravity of intimacy from the husband to the child. This may not seem an overtly sexual manifestation at this time but it disturbs the marriage relationship and every other relationship which touches on or flows from that of husband, wife, and child.

Q. *How can this happen?*

A. Sometimes it happens because there has been some drift in the relationship of husband and wife already. This is not the case in good healthy marriages where people are trying to keep close to one another. They may be surprised to discover the difficulty of doing this. They never anticipated that a child would challenge them to refashion and keep working at their own relationship. But most healthy people are able to react to this and work it through successfully. They grow and are able to give growth to the child because of it.

Sometimes this drift in the mother's attention from husband to child occurs because of circumstances more frequently characterized in the life of the young married people. A husband may be in training for a better job, or continuing his school at night. He may, as has happened on a massive scale in this country, spend several years away at the war. He may, because of economic conditions, have to work more than one job and so be absent from the household just in order to support it. Frequently the child, especially the first born child, becomes a companion to the mother during these times of absence of the father. There can be a strong unconscious sexual component in the relationship. The long range result can be very great and the subtle unsettling of the marital relationship and can have a far-reaching effect on many aspects of their marital life. What occurs at this time certainly builds marital attitudes that will be crucial in later problems connected with the sexual lives of the mother and father, such as birth control or some other form of family regulation. It takes a good deal of sensitivity to be aware of everything that is in the air during this period which is essentially one of growth both for parents and children.

Q. *What are some of the things to which parents should be sensitive at this stage?*

A. The most important overall thing is that they communicate certain basic attitudes which help build the personality of the child or make it difficult for the child to continue growing. What the parents communicate, after all, is what goes into the child's whole attitude toward himself, the building blocks of whether he thinks he is worthwhile or lovable, of whether he is indeed trustworthy and whether he finds that the world itself is trustworthy. These fundamental notions, which can only be communicated effectively by people who are trying to grow toward their own fullness, constitute genuine moral questions.

I don't think parents should become overconcerned but they should realize that what they do affects the learning that goes into the child's own sexual identification and that the way they even express affection has a profound effect on the child. For example, parents may over-stimulate the child because they believe the child is sexually neutral. They really communicate to the child just how much they respect or value him as a separate person.

Q. *You have talked about the continuing relationship of husband and wife as important in the way they relate to the child as mother and father. Does this continue to be significant during the rest of childhood?*

A. The relationship of the husband and wife is indeed important throughout the life cycle both for them and for their children. There are certain stages, especially these very early ones, where the nature of their relationship is crucial to the full personal development of the child. There are many things of which we have an inexact understanding but there are numerous indications that the first years of life have a special importance in laying the foundations for the appropriate sexual identification of the individual child as a man or a woman. The husband and wife are important in this because their relationship creates the psychological climate in which the child achieves very basic learning about his own sexual identity. What I am saying is that if the husband and wife are able to continue to be man and woman to each other through this period of the child's life, with all that that implies, then they will quite unconsciously and without struggle teach the child very basic patterns of self understanding. It is very difficult to make up for this at a later stage of life or to try to teach the child in a more self-conscious or directed way. The rooting of identity from which the later fully developed man or woman will grow takes place in this world of childhood and is strongly influenced, one way or the other, by the behavior of the parents in relationship to one another and to the child. There is a blending of the role of husband and wife and father and mother that does not come off if there is a shift in their basic man-woman relationship. This is a very sensitive area and it seems to indicate to me that one of the most serious moral questions in marriage is keeping the partners in a mature relationship and not letting it slip so that, for example, the father ends up being cared for emotionally like one of the children. This has dire effects on the personal development of the children and on their later ability to express themselves as human beings in their own sexual life.

Q. *What are some of these later problems to which you refer?*

A. I am referring to problems of homosexuality, tranvestism, and transexualism. These are rather broad categories to describe problems which really have very many variations. They seem to arise precisely because of some difficulty in the family situation, especially where the father has not carried out his male role successfully and so has not provided a model of identification for the male children. There are frequently collateral problems that go along with this failed kind of masculinity, problems of alcoholism, gambling, and the like, many of which have a sexual component. When I speak of these problems I am emphasizing the fact that what knowledge we do have seems to point to the influence of the parental relationship in the genesis of these difficulties. These problems, in other words, are the signs, the symptoms in a general sense, that come into the life of persons who have not had normal circumstances of family life in which to acquire a fully developed psychosexual identity. There seems to be some distortion of the psychosexual differentiation in persons who are afflicted with these problems. This occurs during these sensitive years of late infancy and early childhood and they seem to be related to the family situation.

I want to make clear that I am talking about a basic sexual relationship between the husband and wife; this is what must remain clearly the expression of their own masculine and feminine identity as well as of their love for one another. I am not referring to the trends that are somewhat commonplace in our culture and which seem to reflect some blurring of the sexual roles of men and women, such things as the unisex and so forth. I am talking about very basic aspects of the man woman relationship and I am suggesting that a healthy sexual life with each other has great implications, not only for the continued quality of their own relationship and happiness, but for the normal growth of their children. Healthy sexuality has seldom been discussed in these terms under the light of moral reflection. The need for a vital sexual relationship has not been perceived as contributing to the development of the children in this particular way. It is another example of the way that the sexual dimension of life has been isolated from our understanding of our overall development. I raise the question here because I think it throws some light on the fact that the moral questions regarding sexuality cannot be limited as severely as they have been in the past. I think it may be possible that certain moral outlooks de-emphasized the continuing sexual relationship of husband and wife and, in fact, surrounded it with caution, uneasiness, and the nagging possibility that serious moral fault was connected with it. The consequent kind of guilt that circled around human sexuality probably devitalized the sexual life of many husbands and wives, shifting them out of the kind of man-woman relationship that was really necessary for the full growth of their children. If we are to speak of a reverence for life then it cannot be only for the beginning of life. I think we have to go beyond our usual discussion of the purposes of marriage to the point of recognizing how vital the continuing healthy sexual activity of the parents is in maintaining and expressing their man-woman identification and in contributing to the complete development of their children. You must get this into the picture when you talk about what is moral or not in human sexuality.

Q. *Are you saying that some former attitudes tend to de-emphasize the need for continuing healthy sexual activity and that this may have had wider effects, especially on the children, than anyone suspected?*

A. Yes, although I am not surprised that the older perspective was unable to include this. We have learned a lot in this century about man and his sexuality that we did not know before. An overriding moral question, one that is far more important than many other individual aspects of human sexuality, is whether we are ready to integrate what we are learning about man and his sexuality into our whole moral stance. I think that this is precisely what the Christian community is doing and it is from their experience and through their experience that we will learn how to do this.

Chapter Four

LATER CHILDHOOD TO PUBERTY

Q. *Do children have special sexual problems at this time?*

A. I think that it is better to think of this in terms of growth, rather than in terms of problems, although children will certainly exhibit behavior that seems more clearly sexual or sex-oriented during these years. A child is also much more aware of his own person and of the difference between boys and girls. At the same time, he begins to explore the world outside of the home and that, of course, opens up all sorts of possibilities for sexual information and even, at times, sexual experience. He is also busy making friends, learning something that is very important about the establishment of relationships with those outside his own family circle. It is the way all experiences are understood and interpreted for him by the parents, the attitudes which they convey, which really determine whether the child passes through these years in a healthy, growing, and consequently morally developing way.

Q. *Is there any problem with masturbation at this time?*

A. There is plenty of activity during these years which shows the child's concern with his own body and perhaps even with the body of others. I think in the early years of this period this activity is more exploratory than erotic. It is a very human and understandable thing to do; it should not surprise anybody or evoke astonishment or too much anxiety to see a child touching or manipulating his own body in some way, even his genital organs. Some of the habits which children get into at this age do not have a profoundly sexual meaning, although they are certainly aspects of the growing sense of his own person. I think that masturbation as an erotic experience ordinarily comes somewhat later, although there may be some evidence of it during these years.

Q. *What should parents do when they find their children exploring their own bodies or performing what appear to be acts of masturbation?*

A. I think that they should not immediately react as though the child were doing something wrong. All children do this, the parents themselves did this, and children will go on doing it until the end of time. We should not view this with the categories of moral wrong or right; we should rather see these as developmental activities which may need regulation for good manners and for acquiring some sort of self-control, but are not in themselves sinful. These are human activities and they should be understood as such. The important thing is the way the parents react, but I am not saying that they should not react at all. If they are overanxious, if they punish the child for this, they can obviously cause confusion and unnecessary upset in the developing child's life. If they ignore it, they will certainly fail in helping their children to understand and deal with their bodies less self-consciously. Here again, as in almost all considerations having to do with the developmental phases of life, the attitude of the parents is essential. Good healthy parents simply do not make a big deal out of this, but they are willing to ask questions about it and to help the child to acquire the habits that are necessary for good public manners. This demands prudence in all situations that arise at this stage of life.

Far more important is the parents' sensitivity to the child in developing notions of right and wrong, of honesty and dishonesty, and of other fundamental moral ideas which the parents have a great hand in shaping. The parents, in other words, must be atuned to the total development of the child, helping him to integrate anxiety or unnecessary guilt.

Q. *What are some of the things which parents can get over anxious about?*

A. Parents can get anxious about everything from what the child reads to the places he goes to outside the home. All of these concerns, many of which are legitimate, must be handled with prudence rather than a frightened kind of reaction that leads to rather strong and dysfunctional discipline.

If we are to confine ourselves to the area of psychosexual development, there seems to be a great deal of anxiety on the part of some parents that their children should develop in an adequate heterosexual manner. Sometimes these fears or anxieties lead them to behavior which causes the children a great many difficulties in achieving the goal which the parents set for them in this regard. Many parents, for example, have a terrible fear that their child is going to grow up to be a homosexual. Because of this fear, they force the children into styles of heterosexual relationship during the years we are discussing in this chapter. And this long before they are really capable of understanding themselves and their own first relationships to their friends in the new world that they have found outside of their home. Such things as training brassieres for young girls, steady dating down at the grammar school, or artificial and unnatural sex education at this time: all of these betray a problem in the parents which they have in turn handed on, like a defective gene, to the children.

Many children really rebel at being forced into heterosexual relationships at an age when they should be taking a step toward maturity by learning how to make friends with their own sex. This is a perfectly normal stage of development and children should be allowed to go through it with the help and encouragement of their elders. Some of the sexual behavior we see in later teenagers is actually an acting out of their rejection of the heterosexual role which was forced on them in an earlier time of life. One of the theories about the "hairdos" and clothes that make adolescent boys and girls virtually indistinguishable is based precisely on this premature effort to force their growth toward heterosexual relationships. Dr. Ralph Greenson, a Los Angeles psychoanalyst, believes that the heterosexual role has become frightening for these young people and their styles of hair and dress tell us that they are not looking for a lover, someone who is different from them, as much as they are searching for a friend, someone who is very much like them, and in whose presence they can feel safe. Whatever the theory is worth, it does catch the confusion and unfortunate consequences of this parental emphasis.

Q. *What about homosexuality at this stage?*

A. It is not unusual for a child to experience some homosexual contact during these years. This is ordinarily when the first kind of experience of this nature does occur. There is also, of course, a certain amount of heterosexual experimentation that goes on at this time. Not everything that occurs is truly sexual as far as the child is concerned. This will vary from child to child and depend on the rate of growth and development. The outcome of whatever happens, whether the child is approached or threatened by an older person, does depend on the relationship the child has with the parents. This may be, after all, the first time he truly experiences something of his own sexuality. It becomes then a sensitive and important opportunity for the parents to respond to him as an individual, to help him to identify the meaning of this aspect of his personality, and to assist him in integrating what may be a disturbing experience into his life without causing too much later difficulty or disruption.

It is also possible that a child who has some problem with sexual identity may manifest the first signs of difficulty at this age. It is unfortunate when parents do not or will not recognize this, or when they rationalize it away, failing to sense its significance and, therefore, failing to do something constructive about it. Parents frequently do this in sexual matters as well as in situations that have to do with the child's use of narcotics. They don't want to admit that there may be a real problem and consequently fail to provide the child with the kind of help he needs. It is immoral, I think, to deprive a child of psychological help at this very formative stage when it could make such a difference for his happiness and adjustment throughout the rest of his life. A decision of this kind is not an easy one for parents, as there are some events which may suggest the presence of psychological difficulties and are actually part of the fabric of life at this stage. Discretion, thoughtful concern and perhaps professional consultation help to clarify this kind of problem.

Q. *Don't you see a lot of sex play among children at this stage?*

A. Sex play among children is really quite normal. Much of it comes under the heading of exploratory behavior and most of it is certainly not a question of morals as much as it is a question of a natural thing that happens at this stage of personal development.

Parents certainly realize that this kind of sex play does occur and they can discourage it when they come upon it in an understanding and human way. They can avoid some of this difficulty if they make sure that the children have a healthy environment in which to grow up. This includes such things as separate quarters for children of each sex, separate beds for children of the same sex when it is at all possible, and some attention to the child's playtime activities that yet does not go so far as rigid supervision.

It is at this age that the kind of difficulties built into the child by the faulty relationship of the parents may begin to manifest themselves. Immature and undeveloped parents give rise to the same kind of children. That they really were the cause of this behavior at an earlier stage of the child's development now makes it almost certain that they will complicate it by their immature reactions at this later stage, when the symptoms of the child's difficulties may become more obvious. Immature parents, in other words, will not really handle this stage of sex play very well either.

For some sort of viewpoint on it, we really have to turn again to the families with healthy and mature parents. Their own intuitions and common sense guide them in their response to the situations which arise at this stage in the child's development. They continue the process of helping their child to grow by their very presence as truly adult men and women. As they see the child through this stage and through the particular problems that may come up, they are helping to solidify the personality of the child so that sexuality is integrated in a healthy way in his makeup. They give a certain wholeness to the child.

The big moral questions here depend very much on the way that parents handle the situations in which the children find themselves involved.

Chapter Five

ADOLESCENCE

Q. *We know that a lot of changes occur during the period of adolescence. Is there anything that you would like to stress about the sexuality of individuals at this time?*

A. Yes, I think that it is important to realize that, along with the other physical and emotional changes, there is a real transformation of sexuality and its meaning for the individual as he passes through adolescence. The individual is moving now toward adult expression of sexuality and there are profound physical changes involving increased secretions of hormones, changes in the menstrual cycle, and the more fully developed sensitivity that is found in the sexual organs after their fuller development at puberty. We might say that sexuality matures and is of a different kind from that which is found in the years before adolescence. I think we should also say that, although many of the adolescent's problems center on sex or have a sexual expression, sexuality is not the only challenge of adolescence.

Q. *What do you mean by that?*

A. The challenge of adolescence, according to the formulations of Erikson mentioned earlier, is the development of a personal identity. The adolescent, in other words, is working through a mass of varied experiences to define himself and his own unique personality as different from that of his family or his friends. Part of this self-definition, of course, is closely connected with his developing sexuality and his or her capability for an adult relationship with a member of the opposite sex. In the context of this moving toward identity the individual must also deal with restructured relationships toward the adult world and toward the meaning of authority. All of these tasks come under the rubric of overall growth and are affected by the general conditions of life which either contribute to or detract from the general growth of personality. I say this to emphasize the fact that we must not isolate sexuality from the rest of the individual's development or we will fail to see its significance and will only distort it because of our misapprehension. No moral position on adolescent sexuality can be taken that does not include a more general perspective on what it means to pass through the adolescent phase of growth. We must then constantly make the effort to integrate what we know about sexuality with the tasks of growth which the adolescent must accomplish. Only if we keep this in mind can we intelligently discuss any of the individual questions that always come up in terms of dealing with adolescent sexual experience. I think it is important for adults to remain alive to each other. This naturally includes the sexual area of their lives. They will then be much less threatened by the teenager's drive toward independence and his interest in establishing a stable heterosexual relationship.

Q. *Does this identity have any relationship to the identity you mentioned as having its roots in the very early infancy and childhood of the individual?*

A. Yes, in adolescence we find the individual following out the pattern that is really set down in those early years. That is why sexual experience at this time has a significance beyond that which it was given in certain narrow moralistic treatises on the subject of adolescent sexuality. I mean the pamphlets that focus so much on masturbation or on the questions of necking and petting to the extent that the control of these behaviors became almost exclusively the objective of morality. This brought a great load of guilt feelings to persons struggling with their sexuality at this stage and, I believe, made it even more difficult for them to understand their sexuality or see it in relationship to their personal identity. We cannot be afraid of sexuality at any stage of life but it is helpful to remember that as the person firms up his identity he can only do so in terms that are true to his physical and psychological constitution. The adolescent needs experiences with members of the opposite sex in order to solidify the growth to mature personal sexual identification toward which he started moving in the very early days of his life in the family environment. To rule out developmental contacts with the opposite sex, or to view these always with a sense of danger and alarm, is to obscure what is indeed the most important process going on in adolescence – the achievement of personal identity. This is an essential step in the individual's progress through life because it is necessary in preparing him for the kind of relationship by which he will share intimacy with another person. We must see adolescence in this dynamic and progressive kind of way, understanding its importance, especially because of its significance in helping the individual to understand just who he is.

I think it is important to remember that this is a new world for adolescents, that many of them are scared by what they feel in themselves and what they sense in other people around them, and that they need sustaining relationships with older people who will support and understand them even as they give the adolescent the freedom from strict control which is needed for growth at this time. The adolescents find it difficult to talk about what they are experiencing and this makes sensitive older people all the more important. I am not talking about older people who remain adolescents themselves or those other undeveloped persons who seek to revive their youth by jumping back into adolescence. I refer rather to trustworthy older people whose characters and values are established and who can relate to adolescents because they have a feeling for the way human growth takes place. Frequently these people are parents; sometimes other stable adults are very important in this regard. You can think of educators, clergymen, and other significant adults who contribute a great deal to the successful achievement of identity by standing close to adolescents without relinquishing their own maturity.

Adolescence is also affected by certain cultural factors. It has been noted by many observers that the young man who is forced into the world to work while still in his teens and who marries before he is twenty has a very brief period of adolescence. In the United States today, however, with the extension of schooling on a massive scale and with the delay in the pressure on an individual to make himself a part of a profession or the work force, there is an extended period of adolescence. The young man in his twenties who has not yet chosen a career and who still has Graduate School before him may not have resolved some of the psychological aspects of adolescence even though he has completed the physical growth that goes along with this time of life. His identity may not be secure, and his sexuality may reflect this, and his relationships with others surely show signs of it too. It may be useful to keep this in mind as we consider some of the questions about human sexual experience which come up in the course of adolescent development. But no moral position is valid that does not take into account the fact that this is a developmental process which has many levels.

Q. *What about masturbation? Is it a sin?*

A. There is no doubt that masturbation has been considered a sin almost throughout the history of the Catholic Church. It has been considered a sin, or at least
a shameful action, by many men outside the Church as
well. I believe that this tradition of the Church is rooted
in a concern for man and for the proper integration of
sexuality into his personality. I do, however, believe
that, while this concern is laudable, it has been based
on an undeveloped appreciation of man's sexuality and
the overall patterns of human growth. I think we understand man better now and we also have some new opinions about sin. It is not all quite as simple as it once
was. If we try to listen to what the Christian community says about this problem, I think we will catch the
deepening understanding of masturbation as part of the
human developmental process and a moving away from
classifying it as a sin.

  I do not think that the categories of moral right and
wrong are the proper ones to use in trying to understand the meaning of masturbation. When one has em-
ployed these for centuries it is very difficult to move
away from them, clear one's mind, and even entertain
the possibility that masturbation should be thought of in
a quite different light. Unless we can escape from the
setting of sinfulness, we will not deepen our understanding of this problem nor of man in whose life it is
so frequently present. Theologians have surely come a
long way in trying to make it possible to talk about
masturbation as something less than the always-
serious sin which traditional teaching has held it to be.
The difficulty under which the theologians labor, I believe, is that they are trapped by their own categories.
As long as they must consider the question of whether
masturbation is sinful or not, they will use the classi-
fications of sin to discuss this phenomenon. They will

be lessening the gravity of the sin but they will preserve the idea that it is at least some kind of a sin. This is the mentality which I think prevents a better understanding of man and a clearer kind of sexual morality. Masturbation simply does not fit into the category of right or wrong in the moral sense in which Churchmen have spoken about it for so long. It must be considered as an aspect of personal development, a complicated and not easily understood kind of experience, but definitely not something that can be described as sinful.

Theologians and others have felt that once you take away the label of sin, you have excused man of any responsibility at all. Declaring something as not being sinful seems always to be interpreted as issuing a license for all kinds of wrongdoing that we excuse on the basis of psychological theory. This is the outlook which we feel must in some way or another be held on some moral standards or everything will collapse. If masturbation is indifferent, if we do not keep some kind of check on it, then serious consequences may arise. The problem is that we do not have to dismiss masturbation as if it were of no significance when we put aside the categories of sin. Masturbation is important and it is not something which we advocate, as some presumably liberated social scientists do, as a healthful "outlet" for sexual tension. This latter attitude betrays a lack of comprehension of the meaning of masturbatory activities in human growth and development.

We do, however, have to retire the notion that we can only think of masturbation according to the various gradations of sinfulness. We cannot really understand it as long as we keep on impressing this moral template on human activity. We can only misunderstand, misdirect, and, in the long run, fail to contribute to authentic moral development precisely because of this.

Q. *How do you see it as a developmental process?*

A. If we can keep emotional growth in mind, we can
understand that during the period of adolescence the
individual is trying to consolidate all the aspects of his
growth and experience in life so far into some kind of
stable identity. He does this in order to prepare himself for the next developmental step which leads him
into mature heterosexual relationship. It is in the midst
of this process, and with significance for the process,
that masturbation appears in the lives of growing human
beings. It is a source of sexual pleasure, there is no
doubt about that, but if we stop short by looking at it
that way we will miss the other dimensions of what it
means in a person's life. What I am saying is that when
masturbation occurs, it is a sign of a person dealing
with the problem of his own growth. Through masturbation he experiences himself in a new way, catches a
glimpse of an aspect of identity which will have great
importance in the next phase of his development. He
senses himself, in other words, as a sexual being,
whose destiny is to grow toward being able to share
his complete identity in the genital expression of sexuality in marriage. Masturbation becomes a dynamic
kind of event, giving evidence of the individual's efforts
to move beyond the regressive and primitive elements
so characteristic of sexuality at an earlier stage in his
life. It is, in other words, a real sign of growth that the
person is indeed getting himself together in order to be
able to move forward in the life cycle. He is doing
something about his identity in a profound way, achieving a task whose resolution is highly important for his
further development.

It is not because masturbation is so common that we
exclude it from the category of sinfulness. It is rather
because it is a mark of growth, a sign of a person not
seeking illicit pleasure or a disordered experience of

sexuality; it is a sign of a person seeking himself and, in the only way that is available as far as the complicated process of human growth is concerned, he is dealing with a transitional growing together of the sexual dimensions of his personality. It is simply impossible to think of this as immediately sinful. This is not by any means to say that there are no problems connected with masturbation. It is merely to put it into the context of growth and take it out of the context of sin.

Q. *Isn't it possible that it is still a sin in some way?*

A. Yes, in the sense that our basic disposition toward God and other people enables us to commit sins through actions that do not seem at all sinful on the surface. This kind of question, however, brings us back to the categories that we are trying to put aside for a few moments. You only complicate an understanding of masturbation by using a moral category to describe it. This, in fact, has been one of the complicating factors in the whole history of the teaching of the Church about masturbation and man's experience of it in his own life. Men have been drenched with guilt because of the insistence that this human process is always a serious sin. I think this teaching has heightened the sense of conflict in human beings and contributed to a very negative and low self-estimation for many individuals. This has had terrible effects on human beings, confusing them and misdirecting their energies, branding them with inappropriate scars, and obscuring the true meaning of religion, morality, and sexual development.

Q. *If masturbation is not a sin, is it injurious in any way to the individual?*

A. As far as research tells us, masturbation does not

have any harmful physical effects on the individual. This is true despite the incredible folklore and terrible stories about the punishments meted on the physical level to individuals who masturbate. I mean the stories that they would go mad, become impotent, go blind, or have hair grow on the palms of their hands. All these terrifying stories have absolutely no basis in fact, although their effect in making the experience of guilt and terror worse is easy to appreciate.

I think that it is quite possible for masturbation to be harmful to the individual and I think that it is morally dangerous for people to advocate it as a healthy practice or to suggest it lightly as an acceptable substitute for heterosexual activity in adults. These are difficult statements to justify on the basis of what we understand about masturbation in terms of the growth process of the human person.

What is significant for understanding masturbation is the fantasy which the individual experiences while he is masturbating. Now all kinds of things can come vividly into the minds of human beings, especially into the minds of adolescents, so you have to evaluate fantasy very carefully too. When the fantasy that accompanies masturbation is a regressive, and infantile fantasy that keeps recurring in regular fashion, then this is a sign of some kind of serious growth problem in the individual that cannot be dismissed as having no consequences. For a person whose fantasies are of a very undeveloped kind of sexual activity, and which recur in a compulsive fashion, probably means that the person is struggling dynamically against some deep inner block to his continued growth toward maturity. A fantasy of a person committing fellatio on himself, for example, as cited by Peter Blos in his fine book (*On Adolescence,* The Free Press, New York, 1952) as a defensive struggle against homosexuality: "Masturbation," Blos says, "assumes pathological features whenever it consolidates regressively infantile fixa-tions." You cannot shrug off this kind of problem and say that it is a matter of indifference whether the person ever resolves it or not. This kind of problem sug-gests that the individual is blocked because of primary psychological difficulties which, in fact, manifest themselves in the total masturbatory activity. This cannot be disregarded because it prevents the person from moving forward to the next stage of growth. It is, however, a growth problem and there is certainly a moral question connected with that. If speaking about this situation as sinful prevents us from seeing it as something that needs psychological rather than spirit-ual treatment, then this failure in sensitivity is proba-bly a moral fault in itself.

It is also helpful to realize that masturbation can be quite isolating, even where there is not a sign of any deeper difficulty, in that it is frequently used by the individuals to combat depression. If the person grows to depend on masturbatory activities this can also im-pede his development in relationship to other persons. If he finds the locus of all pleasure in himself, then he cannot pass to the genital stage of sharing which is essential to his full growth. This is a more important kind of question to deal with than whether masturbation is in itself a sin or not. We are dealing here with a growth problem and the moral question, as I see it, is whether we deal intelligently and sensitively with this or not.

Q. *What about other sexual activity at this time, such as the problems of necking and petting which have al-ways caused moral concern?*

A. I do not think that you can isolate these experi-ences from the growth cycle either. After all, they are the first efforts, the first reaching out, of one sex to the other and, while this can be exploitative, it can also be a very human effort at relationship, a necessary kind of experience which both tests and helps to define the individual's sense of self and of others. You cannot rule out this kind of activity, and I do not think that Church teaching ever did this completely, although it seemed to take a very restrictive view of what was allowed outside of the state of marriage. This particular mentality, I believe, again reflects a previous view of man which was necessarily limited, conditioned as it was by the general lack of a good understanding of man and his sexuality. There are signs that this view is opening up in response to the community's own sense that not all premarital sexual experience need immediately be classified as dangerous or sinful.

I don't think you can easily say that "anything goes" as far as these activities are concerned either. That is a mindless kind of statement which pays as little heed to the growth process as does the preoccupation with the categories of sin. These activities become appropriate at a certain stage of life when both boys and girls are approaching the time when they will choose life partners in marriage. They cannot be totally sheltered as they become more aware of their own selves, their responsiveness to others, and begin to choose and express the values by which they will live. The moral question in necking and petting has to do with the readiness of young persons for these kinds of experiences. This involves the question of whether they can treat each other with dignity and integrity, or whether, in fact, they are grasping a sense of what it means to be a person and what it means to be responsible for other persons. These are big values that will have lasting moral implications for the individuals involved as well as the families that they raise. This is an important time, a time to form a coherent value system that will bear the weight of their future life experiences. The question that must be kept in mind centers on whether the experiences between the sexes at this age help the integration of their personalities or not. Do they contribute to their moral sensitivity and their responsible use of themselves in relationship to others? Unless these questions are answered there cannot really be any intelligent comments on necking and petting. We will resort to artificial and unsatisfying rules of thumb having to do with various areas of the body with the result that we may miss the meaning of total personality.

Q. *Are there psychological problems connected with necking and petting?*

A. I think many distinctions have to be made before a good answer can be given to this question. Petting can mean many things. It has to do with the area of the body, whether above or below the waist, whether it is above or beneath the clothing of the individual involved, etc. In fact, the young people in high school and college frequently work out a set of moral judgments themselves which strike older people as strange but which have great significance for them. They have a fairly clear idea of what falls within the bounds of sensitive and responsible behavior in relationship to another person. Frequently, in the midst of this kind of exploratory sexual behavior, they will exhibit a strong streak of asceticism, and which they impose in a kind of control that is apparently quite important to them. They may, for example, sleep together in the same bed without any clothes on and not have any sexual relationship. This is by no means uncommon in this age group. It seems to signify their grasp of the importance of physical sharing along with their desire to be respectful and restrained in relationship to one another. In the same way, they make distinctions about parts of the body, and whether the activity is above or beneath the clothing, etc. and they seem to feel quite secure with the judgments which they make. I do not think that adults should immediately downgrade these efforts to handle sexual sharing in an adult way. It is very difficult for youth to understand their experiences and this evidence of a developing sensitivity to one another should not be dismissed without significance. They are struggling for a value system. You can sense it in these efforts to get close to each other while still maintaining some kind of discipline.

This, of course, is not always the case. As a matter of fact, there is a difference according to social class about most kinds of sexual behavior. This suggests that education and other cultural opportunities have a real influence on the developing human person. There have been some studies done on the effects of petting. When it is done heavily and exclusively by young women, there seems to be some later difficulty in marital adjustment. This again highlights the psychological significance of this activity, making us aware of the way such behavior brings us into the overall personal growth and development of the individuals involved. The studies were not well controlled and they do not make a distinction between the girl who engages in heavy petting with several different people or the girl who may engage in it with the same person on a more committed basis. The situation is very complicated but it is clear that petting, like masturbation or any other sexual activity, may have a significance in the growth of the individual that is not immediately apparent. Sex has many uses. Not all of which are for the communication of tenderness or for physical sharing. So these factors must be carefully inspected before we can even be sure of the psychological consequences of this behavior.

Again we have to see the activity in relationship to

the persons involved and, in so far as we can, in relationship to their own life histories.

Q. *You are saying, then, that it is important for adolescents to experience a certain amount of physical closeness with the opposite sex. Is that right?*

A. Yes, I think that the experience of this kind of closeness is necessary for the continued maturation of the individual's sexuality and the successful integration of their sexuality into the complete personality. It fits in, in other words, with the adolescent's job of nailing down his own identity. It is linked closely with the individual's appreciation and understanding of members of the opposite sex. It also confronts the person with the kind of values that he or she would use to guide themselves in the wide area of behavior which we call sexual. It is a time to work through and understand what we mean by crushes and the other fleeting phenomena based solely on sexual attraction. A person must look deeper and deal with the kinds of values that make us truly human, the Christian values, if you will, which we only get to understand through our interrelationships with other persons. This is why Erikson associates the development of the ideals of fidelity and devotion with the period of adolescence. It is a sacred period because the individual voyages for the first time into the deep waters of heterosexual relationships and he must achieve maturity in order to stay afloat.

Not every relationship the individual has during adolescence will be permanent. This is an important truth which must be dealt with carefully. If the growing person is to achieve an understanding of himself and also acquire a grasp for fidelity and devotion to others he cannot be urged to plunge deeply into intimacy with a person with whom he has barely related. I think that it is immoral to push expectations of intimate behavior on growing persons when they are only learning how to handle such behavior. As I mentioned before, however, some parents do force their children into sexual closeness which is not at all appropriate to the overall maturity of the individual. This distorts sex, confuses the persons, and results in numerous other problems such as unwanted children and venereal disease. So we end once again with sex as a non-integrated aspect of personality. It is clear that a certain amount of physical closeness and physical expression is necessary but this must be in accord with the level of growth of the individuals involved and also match and reflect a set of ideals about their own dignity and the words of other persons. Otherwise the experience will be non-integrative, that is to say, it will go against the process of personal growth and obstruct the achievement of identity and the understanding of devotion and fidelity. The old virginity which allowed absolutely nothing must go because this is unrealistic, but the new idea that anything goes is just as unrealistic and damaging.

Q. *What about pre-marital sexual relationships?*

A. I think the same principles apply here. It is interesting to note that moral theology has always condemned these but not with quite the same vigor that it has condemned other aspects of sexual behavior which have not fit into the Christian understanding of man. I am not sure what that tendency in moral theology means, although it may be an important clue to some kind of wise understanding of man beneath many of the moral prescriptions of the past. It may be that there was a recognition of the fact that the sexual expression of love can possibly fit into the lives of persons who are truly committed to one another even before they are married. It is pretty hard to put that into positive law so I think the lesser condemnations may be the only way this kind of signal could have been given by the Church. I think it is a compassionate kind of stance showing an understanding of human beings while at the same time insisting on the ideal that persons who love each other should wait for marriage to express their sexuality.

A lot of people have cited statistics that say there is a tremendous increase in pre-marital sex in our day. Vance Packard did this in his recent book *The Sexual Wilderness*. Others, such as sociologists John Gagnon and William Simon, look at the data and feel that the change is not so great as the statistics lead us to believe. The latter two feel that middle class values still prevail in that premarital sex tends to be kept within the context of courtship leading to marriage. They say it is still attached to a value system which has not altogether abandoned these strengths. They indicate that some element of seriousness or commitment is generally present in premarital sex. This may indeed be true and may, therefore, give some integrity to the experience in certain relationships where the elements of true love and continued caring are present.

I think that it is possible for this to happen but I do not think that we can expect that it will happen in every case. That is the problem, and moral theology must express itself in rules that seem to hold for every case. The Christian community has a certain tolerance and understanding for the problem that we are discussing. This is not to say that it ratifies or validates it but it does, indeed, show an ability to see that this kind of experience need not be totally destructive and that, in some cases, it can be a helpful experience. The decision can only be made on the basis of the same kind of questions which we have put before. We must find out what the experience really means and whether or not it works toward the integration of the persons involved. Does it reflect genuine Christian values, or does it destroy and isolate the individuals who are involved. We have to see what the elements of a good relationship are and deal with sexuality in this context. We know that a good relationship rules out any kind of manipulation or any kind of phoniness on the part of the individuals involved. If these are present in premarital sex, obviously the very use of another person in order to achieve some sort of self-gratifying pleasure is narcissistic and selfish and therefore morally wrong. This happens, of course, in those relationships where there really isn't any consistent caring and where there is no follow-up in responsibility for the other person.

The favorite line used to justify these relationships in a sort of general way goes something like this: "Love is the sole rule of morality. Where true love is present, moral good is also present, despite the objective nature of the action." This is the kind of logic used in what is known as "situation ethics" and it is a highly popular, if not very deeply inspected, line of reasoning. The difficulty is in understanding whether the individuals who invoke love this way really grasp its meaning or its consequent set of responsibilities. All too often this is not the case. What is called love is merely some sort of subtle exploitation which may harm rather than help either partner. The same goes for the slogan which says, "as long as we don't hurt anybody else, it is okay." It is difficult to measure hurt or to be sure that no one is really being harmed by what occurs in premarital sex. If there is exploitation, there can be considerable hurt. This cannot be shrugged off. We know from psychological studies that premarital sex can have many meanings for young people. In some it surely is a sign of their close and developing love for each other. In others, however, it is used defensively to prevent intimacy rather than to enlarge it. This is so because sexual intimacy can be given quickly in order to forestall any possibility that the two persons will really get close to one another. If the only bond they have is sex, then it is a thin and crumbling kind of union at best and that, unfortunately, is the only kind of sex which some undeveloped people do experience.

It is at this age that individuals should learn some kind of profound respect for one another, a respect which does not arise solely from the constraint of legal boundaries but rather arises from the constraint that comes when individuals sense what it means to come close to the boundaries of each other's personalities. There is a constraint that is appropriate for the human person that cannot be lightly dismissed or thought to be of no account. It is the sense of value about the person of another, the comprehension in some way of the inherent dignity of the other person that is the touchstone of all Christian morality. When persons perceive each other truly in a most profound human sense, then automatically a certain appreciation of each other as accepted individuals is absolutely necessary. When people lose the sense of this, which is a sense of their own humanity, then they are no longer capable of any kind of moral behavior. They can only use and exploit each other because they are blind to the incarnate values that are the basis for any kind of mature Christian lifestyle.

It is easy to talk about premarital sex, easy to make a case for it if we don't look too closely at what really happens in the lives of people who experience it. If we did, we might have a little more respect for what is meant by mature chastity.

Q. *Does anyone defend chastity these days?*

A. Psychiatrist Beverly T. Mead has in fact presented an interesting set of reflections on chastity which might be profitably read by everyone in this day and age (*Medical Aspects of Human Sexuality,* January 1970). Mead examines, for example, the statement, "Sex is fun. Why should anyone avoid an easy source of so much pleasure?" Dr. Mead responds that "the boy may find pleasure without complications but, because a double standard imposes social penalties on girls who participate in premarital relations, the adolescent female would do well to be more cautious." He notes that putting the argument this way may seem to reinforce what he describes as the "execrable double standard" but that it is a realistic recognition of the current situation.

The second reason considered by Dr. Mead is expressed this way: "At least I learned something." The difficulty, according to the author, is that what the person learns may be far from the real facts of love. Indeed, the information that the youngster gets from adolescent premarital sexual activity may well be exactly the wrong kind of information and it may lead only to a sense of disappointment and frustration concerning sex. Psychiatrist Mead notes that "sexual activity involves love, a sense of belonging, and a lasting relationship that are elements missing from much premarital sex."

Yet another reason offered by young couples is: "We can find out if we are sexually suited to each other." Here again premarital sexual experience may not answer the question very well. In fact, when sex is experienced in adverse circumstances there may be more frustration than anything else and no true answer to whether the couple are sexually compatible is forthcoming.

Dr. Mead also analyzes the complex motivations that can be involved, noting that the young may be led on an unconscious level by a drive toward emancipation. "By having sexual activities," he notes, "they are proving a point; they are establishing independence; they are frustrating the establishment. This obviously is a way of using sex for non-sexual needs, which may indeed give satisfaction, but may turn out to be damaging to one's developing sexuality." More difficult to respond to is the conviction that is usually stated something like this: "We know each other, we love each other we understand each other; and a sexual relationship is an obvious expression of our love for each other. There may be circumstances which delay or prevent marriage but we do not wish to deny ourselves the sexual part of a loving relationship." Dr. Mead acknowledges the difficulty of giving a convincing answer to this. Such judgments, he observes, are often made by young people prematurely and impulsively, but "in all fairness one may have to admit that such social situations do occur." He moves on to push the case for chastity on grounds that he feels will be more substantial than many of the traditional arguments. Some of the latter are based on old wives' tales, superstition and threats of venereal disease which, because of medical advances, are not quite as powerful as they once were.

In taking a positive look at chastity and its values both for the individual and society, Dr. Mead offers a supportive argument based on a sexual reason. He notes the wide variation in the degree of sexual responsiveness of different human beings and says that this does not seem to be "simply physical or physiological. Our capacity for sexual pleasure or sexual response must be largely a learned or conditioned phenomenon. When a certain activity is considered a very pleasurable one, it is usually because all the experiences of that type, particularly the earliest ones, have been very pleasant and satisfying experiences. It may be that such conditioning applies very significantly to sexual response. If certain first sexual experiences of an individual have been very pleasant, satisfying, reassuring loving experiences which have not been followed by disappointment or disillusionment, then later similar experiences would tend to be just as pleasant and just as satisfying. It does seem reasonable that this might apply significantly to our attitudes towards and our enjoyment of sexual activity. If true, this will offer an important reason for defending chastity. When young adolescents experiment with heterosexual activities, it is often under circumstances which do not allow for the happiest of associations. Excitement and desire may be present but also there is often much anxiety, worry about possible consequences, possible guilt and often a great deal of disappointment about the whole situation."

Dr. Mead notes that the boy in the situation may not feel disappointed with the experience unless it puts him in conflict with his moral values. The girl, however, "is much more likely to be disappointed. She has learned to think of sex as associated with love and may not understand that adolescent boys do not make this association. Consequently, her romantic ideas about the experience as being a wonderful, loving, tender, and exciting one, will not be fulfilled. She may feel disappointed, and in some cases may even feel cheated or used, particularly if the boy does not become more romantically inclined toward her following the experience, and so often he does not."

Dr. Mead concludes that "there may be something to the argument, especially as applied to girls, that an easy surrender of chastity may condition a negative response to a sexual activity later in life. This may be too strong a point of view, although it may be valid to say at least that in later life sexual response and attitudes might be more positive or more meaningful if the early sexual experiences were more satisfying."

Chapter Six

A HAPPY MARRIAGE

Q. *If what you say is true, then happy marriages are important to our overall moral behavior. But what goes into a happy marriage?*

A. Maybe it would be good to take a stand on how we can tell whether a marriage is really working or not and then discuss the factors that make it happy or unhappy.

There is a growing sense of realism in the Christian community that tells us that former, exclusively legal definitions of marriage are not sufficient to express what marriage as a human relationship between man and woman should be. It is hard to believe that two eminent moral theologians could, less than ten years ago, have put so much emphasis on the legal bond that they could write:

> A marriage which produces no children is still a marriage. A marriage which is never sexually consummated is a real marriage. Even a marriage in which there is no mutual help, no life in common, in which concupiscence is not remedied but reigns, where there is hatred instead of love, and complete separation both bodily and spiritually, remains a true marriage in the sense that the essence of marriage is still there; that is, the partners are still married, and in virtue of the essential marriage bond they are still bound to one another as husband and wife (Ford & Kelly, *Contemporary Moral Theology, Marriage Questions* [Westminster, Maryland: The Newman Press, 1963], p. 49).

Now, that kind of emphasis preserves the institution

of marriage by defining it tightly and clearly. It is of very little help to us here, however. Marriages are not so often imposed; man is free to seek out a relationship that will have genuine personal meaning for him. In the present era of freedom there are certain excesses and a recurrence of many experimental styles of marriage-like relationships, most of which have appeared in one form or another during the course of history. But the fact is that most mature and healthy people still want something more than a commune or friendly-arrangement marriage; they want a stabilized continuing union that is properly legalized. The question is, then, what tells us if this legal union is, in fact, a genuine marriage of man and woman truly committed to each other for the long haul of life together. I think that the only truly moral answer comes from our understanding of the principles of growth.

The criterion for a real marriage can only be whether it is a source of life for the man and woman joined in it. If the couple enlarge each other's life and are able to give new life responsibly together, then marriage truly exists. It is life-giving marriage that is essential for the growth and development of morally mature persons. It isn't too difficult to tell whether there is genuine life in a marriage. Anybody with fairly good sense can determine that. I mean life with a little depth to it, not just a superficial, swinging kind of adjustment.

Q. *Do you think that moralists and canon lawyers would accept that idea?*

A. Actually, many of them are trying to approach marriage from the viewpoint of growth rather than the viewpoint of pure legalism. Many will make a good argument, which I will not deny, for legal forms for the general good of society, etc. But, if they want to understand what good people who try to live by the Spirit understand as marriage, they have to look to whether it gives life or not, whether, in other words, the profound elements of love, trust, and responsibility are present in a dynamic way. That is the way the Spirit makes his presence felt in our lives. When the Spirit is there people love, grow, and give life together.

Q. *Marriage is not very simple if we think of it as a process of growth. Things can grow apart as well as together. What goes into marriages where there seems to be life and growth in the right direction?*

A.   One of the most important factors, revealing again the ladder of growth, is that the prospective couple have come from homes in which happy marriages exist. That is one of the ways that truly married people give life; their children are able to move into successful and happy marriages more readily than those who have known unhappy marriages in their own homes.

This is by no means an automatic thing. The reason I believe we see this is precisely because children from happy marriages have assimilated some of the lessons of loving and have an understanding of the kinds of things that go into keeping a marriage alive. The first and foremost of these characteristics is the willingness to keep working and struggling at a love relationship. This vital aspect of marriage is frequently overlooked in anticipating marriage. As a result, the first disagreements and troubles are quite surprising and upsetting. At times people think there is something wrong with their marriage because they have to make such a constant effort to be sensitive to each other all along the way. Actually there is something dead in the marriage where there are no sparks flying from the inevitable abrasions of persons in close contact with each other. Sometimes there is no struggle because the demands are so low and there is nothing much going on in any area, including the sexual.

Q. *Do you mean that it is good for people to fight in marriage?*

A. Well, it brings what is really going on between them out into the open, it puts them in genuine contact with each other when it is a fair and mature kind of engagement. Sometimes couples find that after a real confrontation with each other, which brings out a wide variety of emotions, they are able to enjoy sexual relations more. They have become more attuned to each other in a deeper way with greater sharing of their real selves as the result. The point is not that people *should* fight, but that only people in real contact with each other can have a good fight, and that sticking together to work the problem through because of their love for each other can really deepen the relationship of a husband and wife.

Q. *What about sex in marriage? What are some of the most important things related to that in a happy marriage?*

A. I think couples should realize that their sexual relationship is subject to the laws of growth just like everything else in their life together. Many people have extremely high expectations about the sexual experience of marriage and are terribly let down when they don't exactly light up the heavens right away. A good sexual relationship does not just happen. The couple has to work at this too, trying to be as sensitive and responsive to each other as possible. The burden of making sexuality a significant expression of love and source of communication does not fall on just one partner, although false ideas lead some men to feel that successful sex is all up to them. In fact, a growing and healthy sex life depends on the cooperation of the man and woman. It is a fundamental meeting ground, a profound opportunity for communication, a time when man and woman bring as much of themselves to each other as they can. But sex may only acquire this meaning for a man and woman slowly and they should not be surprised, nor turn immediately to all kinds of artificial aids and other approaches. Neither should they get discouraged, thinking that the situation can never improve. It improves if they keep working at it, if they keep growing together.

Q. What are some of the obstacles?

A. Ignorance, fear, old wives' tales, and immaturity. Ignorance about sex is only matched by curiosity about sex, which, in turn, is only matched by misinformation about sex. It is remarkable that something so common is still so confusing. Nobody likes to seem unsophisticated about sex so people cover up their lack of knowledge or try to keep themselves from feeling embarrassed. That's very natural but it leads to unfortunate and unnecessary suffering. We get an index of how much ignorance there is from the fantastic sales of a book like Dr. David Reuben's *Everything You Always Wanted to Know About Sex (But Were Afraid to Ask.)*

Q. What, by the way, did you think about that book?

A. I think it has a lot of straightforward and helpful information. The author seems anxious to display his own liberation from certain traditional religious ethics and I think he ends up with shifting ground under his feet when he tries to explain the basis for certain things. He seems to use pleasure as the sole reference point; that's an easy and appealing notion but it really is insufficient as an explanatory motive when you are dealing with the human person. Pleasure is a legitimate value for man but it is not the only criterion for his choices, nor is it the highest criterion. To say, "If it gives pleasure, why not?" may be reassuring to some people, but it may not erase more basic problems, nor satisfy deeper human needs that are involved in sexual expression. Pleasure is simply not enough when you are talking about man who thirsts for a deeper significance and meaning for his actions.

Q. *You mentioned something about communication through sexual expression. Is this an area where man searches for more than just pleasure?*

A. Yes, although I hardly want to rule out pleasure as a legitimate and quite healthy aspect of sexual experience. It is just that pleasure never stands alone for long to justify anything that a truly developing person does. Sex should be fun; it should be unselfconsciously playful. It can be none of these, however, if the couple is immature and unable to share and communicate themselves to each other in the other aspects of their life together. Sex is only pleasure, spice if you will, if it does not fit into the context of a good working relationship.

For relatively mature people who understand something about the need to keep growing together, the communication of sexuality attains a profound significance. It fits into the rest of their lives; it is, in other words, integrated in their relationship, and it serves to integrate them as man and woman, too. Men and women say something to each other in sex. It means a lot more than having a mutually good time. It goes way beyond the minimal thinking of the theologians who expressed one of the ends of marriage as a remedy for concupiscence. That kind of talk about marriage, by the way, is the kind of thing that was immoral. Luckily, that rhetoric has been put aside now that the Church has been able to see the mutual nourishment of love as a principal end of marriage. That means something important, something vital according to the whole Christian perspective of things, goes on in sex. When people can really meet each other in their sexuality they confirm, forgive, and redeem each other. They do the kinds of things, in other words, that the Gospels tell us life is all about. That is why it is important to emphasize sexuality as communication. People can be saying the most important things in life to each other. They should understand the language of sexuality well and they should be encouraged to use it freely, not just for the enjoyment, but because so much of what life is all about gets summed up when they are really in touch with each other.

Q. *Can you give me some specifics about communication between man and woman in marriage?*

A. What I am getting at, and what I think the Christian community has truly discovered, is that the marriage relationship, if it is to be a happy one, needs clear lines of communication. That emerges as essential to a happy marriage in all studies of marital effectiveness. Sexuality fits into the whole pattern of experiences through which man and woman communicate; indeed, it brings everything they share into focus in a heightened way. It does that if they are really working at communicating with one another. If they have fallen out of synchronization with each other, if the lines have been cut, then they have little to say to each other sexually. Then sex becomes detached from their relationship, becomes devitalized and withers away both as an activity and a source of meaning. Sex can also become a lot of other things in the kind of communication you see between a man and woman who have drifted apart. It can be used, for example, to express hostility or to humiliate the other party.

So overall communication is absolutely essential to a married sex life that can carry the weight of meanings that are connected with two people trying to love each other as best they can. People do not realize that Masters and Johnson, the famous sex researchers, have recognized this for a long time. Their latest book, *Human Sexual Inadequacy,* reveals the important role of communication for married people. Virginia Masters, the psychologist member of the team, said it as well as it has ever been said, in a recent interview:

> "How superb to be able to regard one's sexual identity with some degree of health and honor, and how lovely to be able to communicate one's needs and place oneself in a give-and-take situation . . . . Primary to truly effective sexual functioning is what we call an exchange of vulnerabilities between partners. This is the ability to be free to give and receive that which you need and desire. In other words, be without defenses, one to the other, because no two people on a long-range basis can have a creative sexual relationship without the willingness to be defenseless. It's an exchange of vulnerabilities (*Medical Aspects of Human Sexuality,* July 1970, pp 40-1.).

I think that you cannot speak of the morality of marriage unless you include the meaning of communication. And we cannot morally respond to the needs of the married unless we are willing to deal with this aspect of their life not just after difficulties arise, but before marriage and during the course of the couple's struggle to understand each other in their married life. There is no doubt in my mind that there was something wrong, immoral if you will, in the undeveloped theology of marriage which formerly emphasized the procreation of children and put everything else in second place. You simply cannot look at man that way and truly understand him or the meaning of marriage. You cannot say sexuality is everything, either. Unless you get the whole relationship into perspective with all the aspects of it carefully integrated, you cannot speak with any moral authority about sex or marriage.

Q. *You mentioned something before about redemption. Is sex redeeming?*

A. Any activity is redeeming if a person gives himself to it with the honesty and integrity which guarantees the presence of the Spirit. Sexual activity is redeeming when it calls forth a response from the couples to give as much of themselves as they can in the context of a relationship where they are working at listening to and loving one another.

There are theological realities encountered in human experience and we have failed, I think, to help Catholics sense how profoundly they are involved in them almost every day. The fact that many of us cannot recognize the mysteries of the Christian life all around us is one of the reasons that it makes it difficult for us to celebrate them properly in the liturgy. Marriage is a good example but it must be taken whole, that is, in terms of everything, including sex, that goes into the relationship.

When I speak about theological realities I refer to the

very basic things that are involved in what we talk about when we say that we all live in Christ. We are joined to the rhythm of incarnation, death, and resurrection – the gigantic reality that makes sense out of our life and our world. Those are not abstract notions, or things we will learn about in another world; they are the things we became implicated in by our baptism and by our efforts to keep open to the Spirit. Marriage, for example, is a continuing source of revelation for the man and woman involved in it. Through their joined experience of life they come to know the depths of the mystery of the In-carnation in a way that they could never grasp on a purely intellectual plane. Something happens between them in a genuinely religious sense as they enter more deeply into life through sharing each other's personali-ties. That is part of the meaning of marriage, that peo-ple get in touch with the Spirit of truth and they grow in relationship to God as they grow in relationship to each other. They begin to grasp the meaning of incarna-tion and, in sex and everything else, they have to face the meaning of death and accept it in order to complete the cylce with new life in resurrection. This Christian mystery is acted out in every marriage, in every good relationship for that matter. It is the larger reality to which we too seldom point while people are undergoing the death of trying to reach and stay in relationship with each other through the love conveyed to them by the Spirit. This very real experience of life in Christ through deepening life with each other is what goes on in marriage. Faith enables us to see and understand it; faith is what helps people who love each other to keep working out their problems together. Sex becomes a sign and symbol of the Christian vision of faith, not because it provides exalted experience but because it so intensifies our grasp of all that is richly human – it helps us to identify our full presence together in the living mystery of Christ. Any moral decisions about marriage must flow from that understanding.

Q. *Do you think most people have any idea of that?*

A. No, I think they believe that religion, Christ, the whole redemptive mystery is somewhere outside them, because that is pretty much the way they have been taught. But they can all identify with the elements of discovery, wonder, and struggle that are in fact our share of incarnation; they understand the pain, the yielding of self, the suffering with no explanation that is crucifixion; and they know the new life that love which has weathered pain and struggle brings - the richer life to the full that is resurrection. They are living the Christian mysteries and we have failed to help them become more aware of it. That is a good example of our failure to integrate the lives of the faithful, a failure terribly intensified by making sexual morality something outside the relationships that are life itself.

Chapter Seven

THE ADULT YEARS

Q. *Are there special observations that should be made about the adult years before we can discuss the moral aspects of sexuality during this time?*

A. The adult years, of course, provide the setting in which the person lives out the truth of his own individuality. It is the time for the expression of adult sexuality and a period of growth marked by the sharing of intimacy with another person. The adult years constitute the time in which we begin to be ourselves. In fact, that might be a good definition for the point in time at which this phase of life actually begins. There is certainly no sharp chronological line one can draw as a border between adolescence and adulthood. When a person consolidates his identity and begins to take on the challenges and the opportunities for self-expression that lie within the realm of adulthood he has entered this phase of life.

Early adulthood is marked by the individual's emergence from the family of his origin into a world which he must now make for himself. This includes the choice of how he will express himself through his profession or line of work, something that is deeply involved with his identity as well as his abilities. Ideally, he has finished all that might be called preparation or education in a very general sense. He is now ready to live, to work, and, equally important to this stage of life, to love intimately. He chooses a spouse and in relationship to that spouse begins a family which makes him responsible now for the growth of new life. This has profound effects on the personality structure of both husband and wife, who have formed a new relationship in depth which makes them independent of the families from which they came and orders their lives to the full growth of their children. A person's life stabilizes around the age of forty, when he or she has a pretty good idea of what they have made of life and what their possiblities for the future are.

Adulthood is the payoff of all our previous growth. It is the time in which a man and a woman make many choices. They can no longer delay these nor live in a world of dreams or fantasy. Neither can they expect to be supported by others or they delay their adulthood so much that they never really achieve it. Adults make moves, all of them filled with hazards and difficulties, which profoundly shape their lives and the lives of many other persons. It is a time full of tests and difficulties, a time in which persons seem to find new challenges as soon as they have fulfilled old obligations. A man cannot enter even the beginnings of adulthood unless he has finished the tasks of adolescence. More and more people, of course, delay doing exactly this. Life, however, lies waiting for them and they cannot postpone it indefinitely.

Sex is an important dimension of adult life. It expresses the maturity of the individual in a way that nothing else does. It tells, in other words, what a person is really like, whether he or she has, in fact, achieved the kind of identity that is sufficient basis for moving into intimate contact with another person. It is at this stage that a person faces and realizes the gospel meaning of life because his interaction with life plunges him deeply into the rhythm of life, death, and resurrection during his adult years. The moral questions connected with sexuality at this period of life cannot be solved apart from the Christian gospel message which has been translated by these people into a saving, internalized faith. In other words, adult life is also the setting for the most profound religious experience. Everything in man is challenged during these years as he faces the meaning of existence. Whatever a man has as a human being must be drawn out and plunged into the swift stream that is life during adulthood. Whatever values a man has now emerge because these are what he looks to and lives by in his decisions about his job, his family, all his goals; sex is a part of all this. Everything comes together in adulthood and the sexual questions cannot be separated from the individual persons, their life histories, their circumstances, and their values, if we are to speak intelligently of them.

Q. *What about falling in love? Does a man really choose to do that or is he motivated by physical or other attractions?*

A. Falling in love is a big mystery. It has never had a satisfactory definition and, as a matter of fact, has not always been directly associated with getting married. People who fall in love want to get married but many other factors have determined who finally does get married. It is probably only in the Western world, and particularly in the United States, where we have tried to associate the processes of falling in love and getting married. It is difficult for Americans, so accustomed to this tradition, to realize that it has not been so and, in fact, is still not so in many other parts of the world. Marriage is arranged on the basis of the wishes of the parents, economic motives, and for reasons of social class. People have tried to get all the pertinent data about individuals, put it in a computer, and match up likely partners for falling in love. This has not worked very well either, because the process of falling in love is not merely the summation of a lot of intellectual material, nor the result of closely reasoned arguments. Falling in love is a very complicated process, with many unconscious aspects, in which the individuals communicate in a subtle way that even they cannot explain fully. It is an emotional experience or, perhaps put in a much better way, a truly human experience in so far as it can be the total response of two individual persons to each other, bringing together, therefore, all the aspects of their personalities. When this occurs in two relatively mature and growing persons, who do not have major psychological disorders, or severe neurotic needs, then the results can be quite happy for both parties. There seems to be nothing like falling in love to insure the kind of strong commitment and strength to continue in relationship to one another that is essential for the adult tasks of married life.

There is a big difference, of course, between true love and the illusion of love. Love can be an illusion when it springs largely from immature and unconscious needs or from some of the other tangled motivations that sometimes lead people into marriage.

Q. *Can you give some examples of what you mean by the last statement?*

A. Yes, and they are familiar to most people. It is not uncommon, for example, to find individuals marrying for hostile reasons. These persons become what psychiatrist Theodore Lidz called "targets of their own animosity" (*The Person*, Basic Books, 1968, p. 404). A young man may be disappointed in losing his beloved and so, to express some kind of revenge, he goes out and marries the first person who comes along. Marriage on the rebound is frequently a disaster for both parties, but it is a self-initiated disaster because it flows from a negative and immature kind of motivation. This also occurs when an individual looks on marriage as a solution to some personal problem. For example a homosexual may marry to cover up his own fears about himself and to establish a certain kind of social acceptance in the community in which he lives. When he chooses a woman he may believe he is getting one who also has a limited interest in sex. This in itself is a pretty poor basis for marriage but, when it turns out that the woman is normal and healthy, the relationship becomes grotesque in the extreme. The effort to cover up a serious problem has only created a more serious one. You cannot leave the unconscious out of this situation. There is plenty of non-verbal communication, for example, between persons who have serious psychological problems and who are looking to express these in their marriage relationship. The classic example of this is the sado-masochistic couple who use marriage as a kind of battleground in which the varied experiences of inflicting or suffering pain of one kind or another actually become the meaning of their marriage.

Q. *Do you mean physical pain?*

A. No, the sado-masochistic marriage may not express itself through the perverse infliction of physical suffering as it is now seen so often in our entertainments. The pain can be a very subtle one, far more psychological than anything else, but nonetheless effective for achieving the ends for which these persons got involved in marriage. In their unconscious they may have a very deep-seated hostility toward members of the opposite sex; what they do is act this out in marriage. In other words, where there has not been healthy growth beforehand, there is not going to be healthy expression in marriage afterwards. It is a very complex business, and we have not given nearly enough thought to these situations in the moral theology that has been drawn up about marriage. I might add that some people who get into distorted marriages do so because these are the only kind of marriages they ever knew anything about. In the family in which they grew up their own parents were united in the same kind of strange union. They seek to reproduce this through their own relationships and they are frequently successful.

Q. *Well, what about healthy people falling in love. How can they tell whether they are really in love with one another?*

A. That is a very common question and we can only answer it in terms of what we have learned from the experiences of mature people who have, in fact, fallen in love. It is on the basis of knowing something about this experience that I try to answer the question.

Man has been pursuing the meaning of love down the nights and down the days of history and he is never sure he has a good grip on it. But, despite the thousand inconstancies connected with measuring or describing it, there is one thing that is sure about love: people who really love each other know it; they know it down deep and they don't need anybody to tell them so. A man and a woman who love each other enough to want to spend a lifetime together know that the way they love each other is different from the way they love their parents, their friends, or even their own children. Real love – the love of one's life, the kind everybody wants but not everybody gets – is unmistakable and a man probably doesn't have it if he has to ask himself too many questions about it. It is a funny thing about the most important love in a person's life. Some people won't wait for it to come, others run like hell when it heaves into sight; still others discover it when they least expect it, after they had given up on ever finding it, or when it is impossible for them, for one reason or another, to express it.

There is a problem in the motivation for love. How many people, we might ask, find and respond to real love, how many actually take the risk that everybody says goes with it? That's one of the signs of real love, all right, but lots of people settle for the security of some kind, any kind, of a marriage, when they get panicked into thinking they will never have any at all. Do some of those smiles on wedding pictures look a little frozen? It may be they are covering the feelings of people who made a bargain for security rather than a marriage, risks and all, out of real love.

Real lovers probably think too much of each other in the sense that they overlook the other's faults. But that's much better than starting out with a well-developed sense of what is wrong with each other, or a heart filled with uneasiness at the prospect of spending life together. It is infinitely better than starting marriage with the idea that if it doesn't work out, one can just get up and get out of it at the first fork in the road. Marriage is filled with roads that split off, tempting the couple to travel separately or just without each other for a while. True love is what makes it possible for people to continue the journey together; and it is making the journey that counts in love. The end of the journey is never important for lovers; they enjoy the trip together more than anything else. A person does not have to be a poet to understand real love. You cannot, however, explain true love anymore than you can explain a poem, or springtime, or friendship. And the more questions a person has to ask himself, the less likely he is to be truly in love. He should remember that when he wonders he should pause; it is a good time not to panic, not to make a bad bargain, or to sell one's self short in a marriage that may not last long. One thing is sure: when true love comes, a person won't have to ask anybody about whether it is real or not.

Q. *You are placing a real experience of love as a powerful source of motivation and sustenance in married life. Is that right?*

A. Yes, love that is mature, that keeps growing, enables persons to face and work through together most of the questions that come up in life. Without love, this is practically impossible. It is difficult enough when people really do love one another. Anybody who marries for a reason other than love had better be prepared for the consequences. Some of these, of course, will be in their sexual relationship, which is such a sensitive key to the whole significance of their life together.

Q. *Perhaps we can discuss some of the sexual problems of marriage. Are there any that are particularly difficult for newlyweds?*

A. I would still put down ignorance as the greatest problem for people in dealing with their sexuality. This is ignorance that has been complicated by misinformation and clouded by strange attitudes. I think we could discuss it on several levels. First of all, there is the informational level. There is simply a lot of misunderstanding about the physical aspects of sexuality. Old wives' tales are hard to kill off. Despite the research and information that have come to us within the last several years, this ignorance is still a very serious kind of problem. I am saying that there is a lack of basic information about the physiology of sex, and a lot of bad information in its place. But then even Freud and Kinsey made mistakes about the physiology of sex.

On another level, there is a form of ignorance that comes because of distorted attitudes, cultural stereotypes, or the restricted understandings that are attached to certain socioeconomic levels of society. We have discussed some of the attitudes which certain churches have helped to generate in which massive and unhealthy feelings of guilt have been attached to a great deal of basically healthy sexual activity. Indeed, I sometimes think that because so much neurotic guilt has been attached to sex, people can no longer feel the healthy kind of guilt which they should experience when they have in one way or another manipulated or misused another person. But ignorance is the enemy and fear sometimes drives people to embrace ignorance rather than to discover the truth.

Q. *Is sex education the answer to this kind of difficulty? Many religious groups seem to oppose it. What do you think about it?*

A. I would begin by saying that many religious groups support sound and integrated programs of sex education. Many of the Catholic Bishops of the United States, for example, have taken a stand in this regard in the last year or so. Sex education, like any kind of education, can be good or bad, depending on the textbooks, teachers, and the attitudes that surround the information when it is given out. Proper sex education, however, when it is carried out with a feeling for the way individuals grow and with a Christian reverence for sexuality as an integrated aspect of personality, can do irreparable good for society.

I don't think we can oversimplify the people who oppose sex education either. Some of them can make a pretty good case against the styles of presentations, the materials, and the teachers involved. I don't think it is ideal, for example, to have a gym teacher or a coach, who may have no preparation whatsoever and may be having marital difficulties of his own, teach the course in grammar or high school. There are many examples where gross lack of judgment has made the sex education course something of a liability rather than an advantage. It can be a very distressing experience if the teacher is immature and uses the occasion to act out his own sexual problems rather than to help the growth of the other individuals. This is not a new problem and, in fact, it can arise in any kind of course in which a teacher may be able to exploit his pupils.

On the other hand, some of the groups opposing sex education do so out of a baseless and neurotic fear which probably stems from their inability to deal with their own sexual lives in very adequate fashion. They run up the flag of patriotism and show the papal colors as well in trying to mass opposition to some kind of sane and sensible sex education. These are also the people who do not want fluorides in their water supply and who seem to see plots and schemes all around them most of the time. I don't think that these people are a good cross-section of the Christian community and it is not their judgment that should prevail in terms of good Christian sex education.

When it is possible for the Christian community to study all sides of the problem, it will invariably vote in favor of an integrated, mature sex education program which is taught with a sense of integrity as well as a sense of values. I believe that the Christian community clearly says yes to this kind of program. In fact, I believe that it is immoral to prevent this kind of education because it is so clearly needed and can prevent so much future suffering in people's lives. A person in the adult stage, with the exploration of intimacy with another person as a challenge before him and who does not have the facts or the values connected with sexuality clearly in mind will have a very difficult go of it. Simple, timely, understanding advice on the part of parents, priests, and physicians can lift away the suffocating cloud of ignorance which has obscured, distorted, and kept us from discussing very basic facts of life. The strange thing in this whole business is that people have suppressed information about sex with the argument that it is immoral and indecent to speak of it. This is clearly a terrible misuse of religious authority, a manifestation of uncertainty and immaturity, and the kind of attitude we have endured long enough both inside and outside the churches. The churches should remember, however, that they can be powerfully influential in clearing the air if they approach these problems with great sensitivity, realizing that you cannot overwhelm people with sexual information they are not ready for, but also knowing that you do not help them at all by allowing them to live in the darkness of ignorance.

Q. *I think we are familiar with the unfortunate kind of guilt which has been built into sex through certain distortions of religion and other values. You mentioned, however, an ignorance that comes from cultural stereotypes. Could you give us an example of this?*

A. Marriages are often severely strained when either the husband or wife approaches the expression of sexuality in accord with some cultural stereotype of what it means to be a man or a woman in this situation. These stereotypes pass from age to age, transforming themselves so they look different although their basic dynamics remain the same.

For example, there is the flourishing notion that the man has to demonstrate his potency as quickly and effectively as possible in the sexual relationship. Indeed, some men look on the sexual relationship as a challenge to their potency, the arena in which they must battle again and again to demonstrate their masculinity. This is a very self-centered approach to sexuality which builds the male image but which leaves the woman completely out of consideration, except for utilitarian purposes. This kind of narcissistic satisfaction motivates men to sexual conquest both within and without marriage. It is not an uncommon feeling to the man who engages in frequent premarital sex. There is no element of sharing, no sign of any understanding or intimacy involved. We might say that the person who pursues sexual activity from this kind of motivation brings no identity to the marriage, that he takes but does not give, while the things that go with mature relationships in terms of sensitivity, tenderness, and concern for the woman, are lacking.

For the woman who finds herself used this way it is a desolating experience. The marriage limited to sexuality of this kind is subject to tremendous strains from within. Frequently such couples will find themselves alienated and embittered. They may develop sexual problems that seem unrelated to this basic problem but which actually spring from it. The woman, for example, may become frigid and, withdrawing from this kind of rape-like sex, communicates defeat to the man who in turn may become impotent. They have destroyed the values of marriage even before they have discovered them. It is this kind of powerful cultural stereotype which causes so many difficulties at the beginning of marriages.

There are other, newer faces to the stereotype, flowing from the new mythology which has reversed the previous example to some extent. In this, the man is driven to provide the woman with a satisfactory orgasm or a series of orgasms. He looks on this as the new proof of his virility. But it is only a slight change in appearance. The narcissism remains undiminished and the effects on the relationship are just as bad.

A great deal of the struggle of modern marriage arises because people think they must keep up to date by achieving what someone writes about as the most fashionable kind of sexual expression in marriage. To be dominated by these outside factors, to think, for example, that orgasm that is not simultaneous is not good, generates tremendous anxiety and tends to disintegrate the relationship of the man and woman involved.

Q. *What about the problem of the average, healthy newlywed couple?*

A. Even the healthiest of people can approach marriage with a certain amount of anxiety – the ghosts of stereotypes still hovering around them. This is not unexpected and should alarm neither husband nor wife very much. Their overall attitude toward sex is important here; the more fresh air that can be let into the experience the better for everybody concerned. The man typically worries about how well he will perform as a husband to his wife. The worries of a woman may be somewhat similar and very difficult for her to verbalize. After all, sex is a form of expression, a new language in which husband and wife are telling something very profound to each other about their relationship and their desires for union with each other. We cannot forget that sex is a language and, like all languages, there may be a little learning needed in order to acquire some kind of fluency. I think that it should be very reassuring for most married couples to realize that they should not expect or demand complete perfection right from the start. They should not ask more from the human condition than it can produce and they should be prepared to help each other to grow in sexual relationship. This will take time, the very thing people are most uneasy about spending these days, but there is no other way around it. Love takes patience and time, sensitivity and understanding. If a young couple can come into marriage realizing this and keep their love and their relationship as the dominant motivation for working through whatever difficulties may arise, they can only deepen and enhance their relationship with one another.

Q. *What about the freedom of husband and wife as far as sex relations go?*

A. I think that the husband and wife, in the perspective of their love relationship and with a constantly developing sense of responsibility toward one another, must work this out themselves. It is very difficult to draw any kind of guideline that will apply very readily in the case of marriage. Married people are entitled to a great deal of freedom as long as this is integrated with the respect for each other and the sense of integrity which their love urges upon them. I think there is a great deal more freedom possible than many married people have been able to experience. The inhibiting factor is ignorance and fear generated by the factors we have previously discussed. The freedom that a healthy husband and wife have in the intimate relationship of marriage is a very precious thing; restrict it too much and you have devitalized something about the marriage; throw away all standards and you have destroyed the meaning of their relationship. Husband and wife are clearly responsible and, the deeper their love is, the more spontaneously will they be able to enter into their sexual relationship.

I think we have to rule out acts which we would normally class as perverse, that is, actions forced by one partner on the other in order to satisfy some crippled aspect of personality. There is a lot of this "sex for every taste" going around in our culture. There is nothing new about it except for the strange rationalization of perversity, such as flagellation, as something supposedly healthy for a marriage relationship. This is primitive and absurd nonsense that can only be propagated by persons with an imperfect appreciation both of the dignity of the human person and the true nature of human growth and development. What is sick and immature can never promote what is healthy and whole.

Another aspect of this is the kind of philosophy so explicit in sex-information books like Dr. Reuben's, to which we have referred several times in this discussion. Reuben provides a lot of factual physiological information that individuals should, but frequently do not, have. I think he gets into serious trouble when he thinks that he liberates people merely through information and through the encouragement to enjoy sex for the sake of the pleasure which he claims is, in itself, sufficient justification for it. This is an apparently sophisticated and extremely liberated worldview of man and his sexual activity; it does not take into account the fact that other values are also important to man and that if these are obliterated, sex becomes an empty and unsatisfying experience. Pleasure is important in sex but it is not everything and it is a poor guide to what sex should mean to a man and woman who truly love, revere, and hope to give life to one another. The idea of having a good time is fine; happiness is, however, different from pleasure and it can never be seized directly, not even in sex. The people who go only for pleasure frequently end up very unhappy. The people who know that pleasure must be tempered by the dimensions of the interpersonal relationship, the people who, in other words, have incorporated the death-resurrection theme in their lives, grow in a very deep and solid kind of happiness.

When a man and woman love each other they can settle a lot of their little problems in bed together. In intimacy they speak the language of sex and find that it is truly redemptive, that it puts them back together when shortcomings and ragged edges have caused abrasiveness. But people who bring immaturity and a faulted identity to marriage, people who seek to take something without even trying to give, find sex an endlessly frustrating search.

Chapter Eight

THE HARD QUESTIONS

Q. *What about some of the questions that have been raised about Christian marriage in recent years, such as those concerned with birth control?*

A. I think that it is clear from the writings of our moralists and from the widespread expression of the Christian community, that the former, extremely rigid interpretation of all acts of birth control as seriously sinful is no longer held with much firmness. I think, as I mentioned earlier in this book, that Catholic moralists are trying to find a way out, so that the change in attitude which seems clear in the Christian community, can be incorporated somehow into what the Church teaches about marriage and sex. It is clear that Pope Paul VI's encyclical, *Humanae Vitae*, has met with a startling amount of non-acceptance because it did not seem to be close enough to the human condition, because it did not incorporate new understandings of man even though it showed signs of recognizing them, and because its basic aim was to reiterate a former teaching rather than to try to develop something new. The moralists now argue about the style of the encyclical, the logic used, and the interpretations possible. They will probably go on arguing until someone has invented a device for birth regulation which offends no moral code. While the argument proceeds, however, we see the Christian community adjusting itself to this pronouncement through a revitalized claim on the primacy of individual conscience in making decisions such as that connected with the regulation of birth. Christian people do not believe that every act of contraception is a serious sin. Good Christians try to work this de-

cision out in terms of their relationship with each
other. I think that this is basically a healthy process
because it means that people are taking their responsibilities toward each other, their families, and the
world seriously. They are attempting to balance these
responsibilities with the ideals proposed by the Church
and to work out solutions which have a heightened maturity about them because they involve so much self-
confrontation and self-analysis. In this process, I think
many married people are becoming more aware of the
kind of values which must guide their marriage as well
as of the realities of the Christian life which they, in
fact, relive through their married life together. It is
clear that many husbands and wives have discovered
a new sense of the Church in their efforts to work
through the problem of birth regulation. They wouldn't
seriously weigh the moral issue unless they were
anxious to keep in relationship to the Spirit and unless
they were willing to accept adult responsibilities. It
is better that they struggle to form their own con-
sciences than that they accept blindly and unthinkingly
a teaching from outside their own intimate experience.
I think it would be immoral for them not to test the
teaching of the Church against what they find in each
other in their married life.

For many people the deepened experience of marriage is a continuing source of revelation. The Spirit
becomes available to them as they open themselves to
each other and to the whole range of experiences which
are theirs on the level of intimacy. This is a continuing
experience of the Spirit's work in this world. He teaches the whole Church in the heart of the marriage relationships of healthy Christians who want to love each
other with a true sense of responsibility. I think when
people strive to live by the Spirit, follow the voice of
their conscience as it has been informed both by the

world around them and the acts of the Spirit Himself, then we have to respect and learn from this occurrence.

The only moral position we can take about birth regulation is one that refers it to the judgment of husband and wife. They must be sensitive to each other, the teachings of the Church, the traditions of their culture, and the multilevel circumstances of their lives. What ultimately will help them to decide is a sense of values that they bring to their relationship together. The decision they are asked to make is not easy. It cannot be dismissed easily nor smoothed over with generalizations which do not take into account the elements of struggle which are integral to these decisions. Morality is found in this kind of struggle rather than in the prefabricated decisions which eliminate the need for struggle altogether.

Married persons cannot make any decision without reflecting what they mean to each other, what they hope to mean to each other, and an understanding of the true motivation for any decision they make in regard to their sexual life. I think it is possible for a couple, for example, to refuse to have children because of inadequate and undeveloped motives. The moral problem here is their self-centeredness, their withdrawal from the challenges of life, and the reasons that lead them in this direction. I think it is possible to rationalize away birth control with noble sounding statements which actually cover up an inability to love in a truly profound and life-giving fashion. These motivations, of course, cannot possibly justify a choice of birth control as a method of regulating family size.

There are deeper things involved that have not frequently been discussed in the many problems associated with birth control. Purely on psychological grounds, we are in danger of doing something that may be harmful to man if we lightly dismiss the importance of man's genital sexuality in bringing new life into the world. Eric Erikson has commented on the human frustration that is implicit when we limit fertility. The whole aim of many psychiatric and psychological theories is to move man through the developmental stages of life to the crowning maturity which is generally agreed upon as that time when he can exercise his genital sexuality. In other words, the capacity for heterosexual relationships is the last stage of growth in the person's development toward maturity. Now to lead a man up to that stage and then to prevent him from generating new life may well distort his personality. As Erikson notes in an intereview: "I would go even further . . . and say that Freud, by paying so much attention to the pre-pubertal impediments of the genital encounter itself, underemphasized the procreative drive as also important to man. I think this is a significant omission, because it can lead to the assumption that a person graduates from psychoanalytic treatment when he has been restored to full genitality. As in many movies, where the story ends when lovers finally find one another, our therapy often ends when a person can consummate sexuality in a satisfactory, mutually enriching way. This is an essential stage but I would consider generativity a further psychosexual stage, and would postulate that its frustration results in symptoms of self-absorption" (Richard L. Evans, *Dialogue with Erik Erikson* [New York: Harper & Row, 1967], p. 52).

I think it is important, if we consider man in developmental sequence, to keep this in mind. People who rule children out of their lives may also be ruling full growth out of their own lives. They may be denying themselves the fulfillment that they think they can find if they do not take on the obligations of children for one reason or another. What all this comes down to is the need for a very careful self-examination, the need to appreciate as deeply as possible the many stages of personal growth, and the fact that man's sexuality has a significance that it may lose if we do not see it in the perspective of overall life and growth. I don't think that any decision connected with love and marriage is an easy one; the values involved are quite complex, and husband and wife must take seriously their obligation to work out their relationship with each other and with the family they nurture with as much integrity and with as much openness to the Spirit as possible. More important than any of my reflections, however, is the fact that the Christian community is, in fact, doing pretty much what I have just described. I think we will learn from this and that the official teaching of the Church will be amended by this manifest collegial response of the community to the more traditional position.

Q. *What about divorce? Do you think that this has to be entertained as a possibility by the Church?*

A. I think the Church is entertaining this as a possibility, just as it has always, in certain circumstances and under certain conditions, put an end to marriages, even validly contracted ones. There is a growing realization on the part of many moralists who have been listening to the Christian community that an absolute application of the indissolubility of marriage, while it reinforces a very high ideal, does not match human experience and man's understanding of the true meaning of marriage. We have discussed many examples of distorted motivations for entering marriage in previous questions. I think it will be difficult to prove that any real marriage existed in some of these cases. There was no life and no capacity to give life. There was only destruction and alienation. You cannot call these unions by the name marriage. Members of the Christian community are quite aware of the truth about marriages in which no life exists, even as they know all too well the tragedies that distort the lives of the children who come from these non-marriages. Recent statements by certain Canon lawyers indicate their broadened understanding of the factors that can put a marriage to death or prevent it from ever having even known the breath of life. There is movement, in other words, even within the official Church to dissolve the bonds of these marriages. People have been suffering as they have been waiting for these developments to occur. I do not think there is any doubt but that a more compassionate understanding of the factors which invalidate marriage will be gradually incorporated into the practice of Church courts even as the transformation of the Church laws moves more slowly around it.

It is difficult to condemn Church lawyers who are striving to bring the marriage legislation of the Church up to date. Theirs is a difficult, almost an impossible task, when you consider the complications involved in this kind of process. What they are doing, however, is catching up with the general Christian awareness that a ceremony does not make a marriage, that the legal bond does not sum up everything the Church has to say about human love and life, and that something obviously has to be done about it to protect the individual freedom of Christians and the dignity and meaning of married love. The official Church is moving in this direction; the People of God are there already.

Q. *Where do you think the Christian community stands on the question of abortion?*

A. I think that there is a pretty heavy judgment against it among Catholics; the long-time tradition of supporting life and giving it proper reverence asserts itself rather clearly. There is very little dissent or conflict in the Catholic community on the question, practically nothing compared to the reaction to *Humanae Vitae.* There is, however, the beginning of a discussion that will surely develop considerably during the next ten years. It would be helpful to make a close study of the way this discussion develops. We would learn a great deal about the process of dialogue within the Christian community as well as about the manner in which what takes place in the Christian community reaches and affects official teaching positions of the Church.

Daniel Callahan actually set the lines of the discussion in his recent book *Abortion: Law, Choice & Morality,* Macmillan, New York, 1970. He shows how the Church has consistently defended the right to life and how this principle has been central in the Catholic thesis against abortion. Callahan reflects also, however, on the fact that, in certain other circumstances, the Church relativizes this right to live as, for example, in the defense of a just war in which many innocent lives are sure to be taken. He believes that the right to life, vital and important as that is as a moral consideration, has been isolated in Catholic teaching from other rights. The discussion, Callahan believes, will center on putting these rights in relationship to one another and working toward an answer in the environment of tension that is thereby created. In other words, to put the question in moral perspective, he believes that the fetus's right to life is only one among many rights that must be balanced against each other; and that this has not been done in practice. He tries to underscore the tradition that prizes life while placing the moral decision in the hands of the woman who must look at many values and duties while she makes her decision. He says, for example:

The bias of the moral policy implies the need for moral rules which seek to preserve life. But, as a policy which leaves room for choice – rather than entailing a fixed set of rules – it is open to flexible interpretation when the circumstances point to the wisdom of taking exception to the normal ordering of the rules in particular cases. Yet, in that case, one is not genuinely taking exception to the rules. More accurately, one would be deciding that, for the preservation or furtherance of other values or rights – species-rights, person-rights – a choice in favor of abortion would be serving the sanctity of life. That there would be, in that case, conflict between rights, with one set of rights set aside (reluctantly) to serve another set, goes without saying. A subversion of the principle occurs when it is made out that there is no conflict and thus nothing to decide (p. 501).

I do not think that the Christian community has yet struggled deeply with this line of reasoning but I believe that it is preparing to do so. I am not referring to rationalizers or others looking for an easy out to indulge the affluent (who profit most from abortion reform although they argue for it in favor of the oppressed poor, the latter being generally excluded from the presumed benefits of abortion reform because of the high costs involved). I refer rather to those conscientious Christians who know, because of the scars of life they themselves bear, that life is indeed complex and cruel, and that simple answers on either side of any question are hardly to be trusted. In other words, I think we have to entrust this question to the Christian community which can reflect on theological teaching in the light of its own experience. That is what will happen in the years to come.

Q. *You mentioned something about rationalizers. Do*

you think that most of the arguments for abortion come from people looking for an easy and undemanding morality?

A.   No, that would be an unwarranted judgment on the many sincere people who have tried to think through the problems connected with unwanted children, illegal abortion mills, and other grisly aspects of the question. They are not all unprincipled people by any means. They are, however, as there are on many questions, sloppy and sentimental thinkers as well as individuals who make their moral decisions on the basis of what gratifies them. There is a certain danger, as many have pointed out, that we may damage or endanger our overall respect for life if we too hastily come to a decision in favor of abortion without proper reflection and self-confrontation. These are, after all, indispensable elements in any mature moral decision. I think Callahan says this very clearly in his book and that is evidently the process he went through himself in writing it.

There *is* a lot of sloppy thinking on the subject. For example, the notion that the decision is solely between a woman and her doctor. This clearly truncates the relationships which are important values to be understood and preserved.

Q.   *Could you explain what you mean about abortion not being a matter solely between a woman and her doctor?*

A.   I would like to talk about that a little because it is a good example of the catch-phrase used as a substitute for the painful self-search that really must be a part of serious moral choices.

Between a woman and her doctor is certainly one of the most fashionable phrases; it is uttered with varying inflections by different groups who champion more liberal laws for what they describe as "the termination of pregnancy." The phrase, pointing to where the decision about ending pregnancy is supposed to reside, is spoken solemnly, almost piously, by some abortion reformers, as though they were in the habit of turning away at the most delicate moments of life as a sign of their respect for the individual. The same phrase is spoken with more feeling by the members of Women's Lib who use it as part of their definition of female independence from male domination. It is even spoken by dewy-faced actresses and other assorted celebrities on interview programs; you can almost hear their press-agents at their elbow, like lawyers rehearsing a client, feeding them the line and saying, "Baby, you want to look liberated, then you got to say this."

Part of the point of the statement is, of course, that it is very difficult to legislate moral decisions for a society that has many levels of religious belief and ethical conviction. One can hardly doubt that; but, if we are interested in man and his fulfillment, we ought to test the phrase for logic, consistency, and for its long-range implications. It is clear that it is a phrase that sounds good; it is practically a visa for travel through some of the liberal geography of our day. It is especially useful if you are not inclined to think of, or if you want to head off, a discussion on a hot topic before it begins. There have been other phrases used for the same somewhat self-protecting purpose. You remember that one about the race question, don't you? The one that went (and in some places still goes), "I say give the Negroes twenty years and they will settle the problem themselves." This style of comment implies a liberal philosophy but, in truth, it exempts the person using it from thinking through and taking a stand on his own. Maybe it is all right to avoid arguments once in a while, but let's not fool ourselves when we do it.

Far more serious, however, than the pseudo-liberal dodging of the issue built into such phrases is the question of whether there is any truth in the claim that the decision to end pregnancy belongs only to a woman and her doctor. This leaves the husband and prospective father out of the problem altogether, freeing him from something for which he has just as much responsibility as the woman, even if we restrict our understanding of it to the basic biological facts. But this question entails a great deal more than just biology; it includes some of the most solemn issues involved in being a person. Among these are the nature and demands of mature relationships between men and women, the shape and future of marriage and the family, the nature of love, and the power of certain professional people in the most intimate areas of our lives.

To place all the burden for a decision about abortion on the woman is to separate her from her relationship to man, to alienate her, if you will, from the relationship which needs deepening rather than narrowing in our time. If a woman's body is a castle in which she lives fundamentally alone, then she is inviting siege and pillage more than peace and love. Men and women are meant to build a life and grow in love together; there cannot be an area of such mutual significance that can be suddenly and abruptly closed off. A decision made outside of relationship to each other breaks the partnership along the very seam of intimacy, shutting a couple off from the kind of healthy concern for the future that is a sign of genuine love. It also takes away from the man something he cannot even give away: his responsibility for his own sexual behavior. To exclude him from any decision that clearly involves him in such a weighty manner is to give him an undeserved sense of freedom, an open ticket for the progressively isolating journey to the land where all the tireless playboys go to die.

Also, we might begin to wonder whether the medical doctor either wants or deserves the partnership he is being given in the decision about abortion. Indeed, with no disrespect to the dedicated medical profession, it is clear that the mantle of moral judge is wrongly being given to doctors for many issues connected with basic human values and rights. The medical doctor may need a measure of demythologizing before we cede to him the functions of philosopher and moral theologian. The typical doctor knows this and tries to restrict himself to the medical aspects of most decisions with which he is involved. But society is pushing him hard to take on responsibilities for which he is hardly prepared at all through his training (which includes lots of anatomy, precious little psychology, and hardly any ethics). And, despite the demigod image of the television physician, doctors have severe problems themselves. The pressures are great, and so is the suicide rate; often the hours are long and erratic, which can be a disruptive factor in their home life. In fact, medical men need added support and understanding from clergymen and others who could assist them in bearing the weight of the many human decisions in which they become involved every day.

To leave abortion as a matter between a woman and her doctor is to distort the basic relationship of husband and wife. It is even to erase the mutual responsibility that is still a part of other man-woman relationships, howsoever casual or brief these may be. There are consequences for what we do and now is the time for intensifying our awareness of this easily disregarded fact. To put all the burden on the woman is to eclipse further our understanding of man-woman relationships and validate an everlasting adolescence about sex in the men of the land. And before we make the doctor, or anybody else, the new arbiter of our morality, we ought to inspect his credentials and see whether he possesses the sensitivity to human values necessary to be a part of basic decisions about life and death. Believe it or not, morality does have something to do with things other than war and crime; it begins at home, in the responsibility that men and women assume for each other and for the future of the world.

Q. *What about the problem of homosexuality? Do you think that this is a moral or a psychological problem?*

A. Basically, homosexuality, a word that can have many meanings, is a developmental psychological problem that we are just beginning to understand. Indeed, for perhaps the first time in history, the Christian community has been able to look at this problem as something more complex than mere perversion. For centuries homosexuality was regarded almost exclusively as a practically unspeakable moral problem, an unsightly human sore that was cauterized by moral outrage and indignation. But we have learned a lot about men in the last century, enough to know, for example, that those who professed the greatest disgust for homosexuality were sometimes defending themselves against their own fears about their sexual identity. We now know that homosexuality seems to be a problem of growth that is related to the early experiences of the individual in relationship to his or her parents. The subtle interactions of the early years, so closely interwoven with the relationship of the husband and wife who are the mother and father, profoundly shape the gender identity of the young child. We discussed this in earlier chapters, suggesting that the real moral question lies in responding to the needs of the parents who may be having difficulties with their own relationship and, therefore, may be setting the scene for a problem for their children. There is much that we do not understand about homosexuality, but we know enough to say that, as a disturbed psychological condition, it can hardly be classified as a sin.

That does not mean that homosexuals are freed from the restraints of morality insofar as they can be helped to observe them. For example, there is no excuse for the manipulation of others that homosexuals sometimes freely engage in as though it were of no consequence. There are moral questions involved, and, as a matter of fact, a clear responsibility for the Church to educate people properly both in understanding homosexuality and in helping homosexuals to understand themselves. Those people who think *gay is beautiful* are cruelly deceiving themselves; those people who believe homosexuals constitute just another minority group are trying to change sickness into health.

Homosexuality, the conditions that give rise to it, the many problems connected with it - the principal moral question lies in illuminating these issues with compassion and understanding. I believe that the Christian community has moved a long way in this direction, making a genuine moral response, in other words, to a painful human problem.